NICOLA GRAIMES

NEW VEGETARIAN KITCHEN

raw / grill / fry / steam / simmer / bake

DUNCAN BAIRD PUBLISHERS

LONDON

For Silvio, Ella and Jool, with love.

NEW VEGETARIAN KITCHEN
Nicola Graimes

First published in the United Kingdom and Ireland in 2011
by Duncan Baird Publishers Ltd
Sixth Floor, Castle House
75–76 Wells Street
London W1T 3QH

Conceived, created and designed by
Duncan Baird Publishers

Managing Editor: Grace Cheetham
Editor: Nicole Bator
Designer: Luana Gobbo
Commissioned photography: William Lingwood
Photography Assistant: Isobel Wield
Food Stylist: Bridget Sargeson
Food Stylist Assistants: Jack Sargeson and
  Katy McClelland
Prop Stylist: Wei Tang

British Library Cataloguing-in-Publication Data:
A CIP record for this book is available from the British Library

ISBN: 978-1-84483-936-0

10 9 8 7 6 5 4 3 2 1

Typeset in Conduit, Bodoni and Filosofia
Colour reproduction by Colourscan
Printed in China by Imago

Publisher's note: While every care has been taken in compiling the recipes for this book, Duncan Baird Publishers, or any other persons who have been involved in working on this publication, cannot accept responsibility for any errors or omissions, inadvertent or not, that may be found in the recipes or text, nor for any problems that may arise as a result of preparing one of these recipes. If you are pregnant or breastfeeding or have any special dietary requirements or medical conditions, it is advisable to consult a medical professional before following any of the recipes contained in this book.

What is a vegetarian?
A vegetarian is someone who does not eat meat, poultry, seafood or other animal-derived by-products, such as gelatine.

Notes on the recipes
• Cheese, especially those made using traditional methods, may contain calf rennet, so check labels first. Look for 'suitable for vegetarians', the 'V' sign or 'contains vegetarian rennet' on the label. All cheeses used in the following recipes are available in a vegetarian form.

Unless otherwise stated:
• Use medium eggs, fruit and vegetables
• Use ripe fruit and fresh herbs
• Use unsalted butter
• Do not mix metric and imperial measurements
• 1 tsp = 5ml • 1 tbsp = 15ml • 1 cup = 250ml

Acknowledgements
My sincere thanks go to Grace Cheetham for commissioning me to write this book and for her continued enthusiasm and having faith in me. Thank you also to my fantastic editor, Nicole Bator, who was a huge inspiration and generously shared her talent, and kept me going with her positive feedback. I would also like to express my huge gratitude to the rest of the team behind the book, designer Luana Gobbo, William Lingwood for the great photography, food stylist Bridget Sargeson and props stylist Wei Tang.

CONTENTS

INTRODUCTION

This book has been a long time in the making. What began as a little seed of an idea many years ago has evolved and developed into a collection of recipes that I couldn't be more excited about sharing. Gone are the old stand-bys long associated with vegetarian food. In their place are fresh, modern recipes that broaden the appeal of meat-free cuisine, giving vegetarians lots of new ideas and tempting even the most adamant meat-eater with adventurous, irresistible flavours.

I came to cookery writing in a back-to-front sort of way, from my time as a food editor with a love of cooking to being given the wonderful opportunity to write my own book many years ago. But vegetarian cooking has always been a passion, and I love the challenge of planning and developing a dish. For me, vegetables are too often considered an afterthought, plonked on the side of the plate, playing second fiddle to the other foods they're served with. And too often, a vegetarian 'meal' is unbalanced, with lots of carbohydrate but little or no protein. That's why this book focuses primarily on recipes that are 'complete' meals in themselves, with both a protein and carbohydrate, rather than a collection of insubstantial side dishes.

Truth be told, I didn't really want this book to be classified as a 'vegetarian' book. It's more a celebration of the ingredients I love, from fresh produce, herbs, spices and pulses to grains, nuts, cheese, eggs and more. It's the quality, nuances and versatility of these foods that I wanted to highlight, and the fact that the recipes happen to exclude meat, poultry, fish and seafood is really just incidental.

I'm actually quite an impatient cook and most the of time I just want to create something delicious and, usually, nutritious, as easily and quickly as possible. Many of the recipes in this book satisfy these criteria, but they're balanced with others that take a little more time and effort. Either way, the principal aim is to get the best out of ingredients by exploring different ways of preparing and cooking them. Presentation is also key. This doesn't mean spending lots of time fiddling with food on the plate but, more importantly, thinking visually and considering how ingredients work together in terms of colour, texture, flavour and temperature. It can be as simple as sprinkling some fresh herbs or crushed, toasted nuts over a dish to add colour or crunch.

The cuisines of the world are a huge inspiration to me, so you'll find recipes influenced by dishes from as far afield as Japan and Indonesia to Italy and the Caribbean — all with a contemporary, and sometimes a fusion, twist. I created all of the recipes for the home kitchen, and even the most novice cook is guaranteed to succeed with them. If you're already quite confident in the kitchen, the recipes will provide you with a fresh approach and plenty of new ideas to start trying.

ABOUT THIS BOOK

Understanding the basics about cooking techniques gives you great freedom to experiment, be creative and bring out the best in the ingredients you use. Choosing to grill, steam or fry an ingredient, for example, will alter its taste, texture and appearance. Take an onion: slow-cooking curbs its pungency and gives it a meltingly soft texture, while stir-frying results in a slightly crunchy and more intensely flavoured taste, and a raw onion is crisp and sharp.

New Vegetarian Kitchen highlights the six core techniques you'll use to make outstanding meals: raw, grill, fry, steam, simmer and bake. Each one has its own benefits and idiosyncrasies. Most ingredients are better suited to certain cookery techniques than to others, so the basics of each technique are explained in the following pages and the recipes show you which ones to use when. Of course, many recipes are a combination of different techniques that work in harmony to create a finished dish. When more than one method is used in a recipe, the recipe is found under the primary technique.

This is not a handbook to cookery techniques but rather a showcase of the possibilities that each technique presents. It's about being adventurous and playing around with flavours, colours and textures to make sensational meat-free meals. I've also included guidance on how to cook certain ingredients, such as rice and dried pulses, and there's a handy glossary you can refer to if you're baffled by any of the more unusual ingredients featured in the recipes.

RAW

Bright and vibrant in colour, crisp and crunchy in texture, and quite different in taste to cooked dishes, meals created with uncooked ingredients can be surprisingly diverse and inspiring. By experimenting with marinating, grinding, blending, chopping, slicing and freezing foods, you can create a stunning array of dishes that are colourful, fresh and nutritious. This chapter focuses on getting the best out of uncooked ingredients, whether it be a garlicky Chilled Almond Soup or a Savoury Cheesecake with Red Pepper and Coriander Relish.

It's common sense, but so often forgotten, that variations in texture and consistency influence taste and also affect the way an ingredient integrates with others on a plate. For example, preparing a raw carrot in myriad ways can produce varying end results: a thickly sliced carrot tastes quite different from one that is coarsely grated, puréed or juiced.

Being adventurous with presentation contributes to a dish's overall success, too. Preparing fresh fruit and vegetables, nuts, seeds, herbs and spices in different ways enhances their visual impact on the plate.

Many of the dishes in this chapter adhere to the principles of the raw food diet (broadly defined as foods that are uncooked or warmed to a temperature no greater than 40°C/104°F). Others feature a main ingredient that is uncooked but may be combined with cooked foods, such as canned beans or cheese to add extra substance and complement the raw ingredients. Even though there's no full-on cooking in these recipes, they will offer you new ways of combining raw ingredients to make delicious meals.

GRILL

Grilling relies on applying intense, dry heat from above to the surface of a food and is used to quickly brown or caramelize. It lends a dish a slightly smoky, toasted or barbecued flavour, depending on what you are cooking. In fact, the grill is sometimes used as an alternative to the barbecue.

Successful grilling is influenced by two things: temperature and the distance the food is placed from the heat source. The dry, intense heat of a grill is perfect for a number of things. You can brown the top of a gratin or pie or finish cooking dishes such as a frittata or Spanish tortilla. Grilling is also great for melting cheese and giving a golden glaze to marinated vegetables, fruit and tofu. Grilling also provides a healthier, low-fat alternative to frying foods such as burgers and fritters.

Certain cheeses, particularly halloumi, mozzarella, goat's cheese crottin and feta, are especially suited to grilling since they melt, soften or brown but still retain their shape. Aubergines, peppers, courgettes, mushrooms and tomatoes are just a few of my favourite vegetables for grilling. I slice them fairly thinly, brush them with oil and grill until softened and charred in places. Grilling vegetables this way is often much faster than it would normally take to roast them.

Apples, pears, peaches, pineapple, mango, bananas and many other fruits – perhaps with the exclusion of berries – are suitable for grilling as well, since the dry heat helps to caramelize the sugars found naturally in the fruit. Preheat the grill until very hot, then sprinkle the fruit with caster sugar or drizzle with honey and arrange it in a single layer on baking paper. Position the baking sheet about 7cm/3in from the heat and grill until softened and golden – deliciously simple.

FRY

There are many variations of frying, each dependent upon the quantity of oil, the level of heat, the type of pan used and the amount the food is stirred or tossed in the pan during cooking.

Sautéing is great for cooking small, evenly-sized pieces of food quickly in a little oil or butter, tossing them regularly until browned. A wide, shallow pan with straight sides is perfect for this technique. The fat should be preheated in the pan over a medium-high to high heat until it is 'shimmering' but not smoking (butter will become foamy). If the fat is too cool, then whatever you are sautéing will not brown and may absorb the fat, becoming greasy. Use just enough oil to coat the base of the pan and when hot, add your ingredients and toss until golden and beginning to crisp – if they start to burn, reduce the heat slightly. For the best flavour, try using a combination of oil and butter but, depending on the style of cooking, adapt the type of fat you use, using olive oil in Mediterranean dishes, for instance.

Pan-frying uses slightly less heat than sautéing (medium to medium-low) and only a small to moderate amount of fat. It is more suitable for larger pieces of food that don't require constant stirring but are simply turned over occasionally.

Griddling differs from other methods of frying in that the food, rather than the pan, is oiled, which ensures the characteristic seared or charred marks and the wonderful slightly smoky flavour of griddled foods. When buying a griddle pan, make sure it is made from heavy cast iron so it can be heated to a very high temperature without buckling. It should be heated before adding food so that the heat sears the outside almost straightaway but retains moisture inside. Vegetables take on a new dimension when griddled, as do tofu, tempeh and halloumi, which hold their shape during cooking. Thick slices of griddled bread drizzled with oil, rubbed with garlic and topped with tomato make the perfect bruschetta.

Shallow-frying is used for browning the outside of foods such as vegetable fritters or burgers, while sealing in moisture and flavour. It uses more oil than sautéing, pan-frying or stir-frying. The food being cooked is half-submerged in hot oil and is normally turned over halfway through cooking. It's a good idea to cook the 'presentation' side first for the best appearance. A heavy-based frying pan is best for shallow-frying since it ensures even heat distribution.

Deep-fried foods should have a crisp, golden exterior and tender centre – they should never be greasy or soggy. Deep-frying is ideal for cooking foods such as doughnuts, fritters, gyoza and potatoes, and for things coated in batter or breadcrumbs. In this quick method of cooking, the food should be completely submerged in the hot oil. The right type of oil is crucial: sunflower, groundnut and rapeseed oils are ideal because of their mild flavour and high smoking point, which means they remain stable when heated to a high temperature. The oil temperature is also important to ensure that the centre of the food is cooked and the exterior crisp but not burnt. Use a kitchen thermometer to monitor the temperature as you heat the oil, or try the bread test: heat the oil until it gives off a smoky haze, then drop in a cube of day-old bread and time how long it takes to brown. The list below explains the approximate time it takes to brown the cube of bread.

- Low heat: 60 seconds = 170°C/325°F
- Medium heat: 40 seconds = 180°C/350°F
- High heat: 20 seconds = 190°C/375°F

The size of the pan you use when deep-frying is also important. Choose one that has deep sides but isn't too large. Importantly, do not fill it more than two-thirds full with oil. If using a basket, dip it in the hot oil before adding the food to prevent the food from sticking to it. After cooking, remove the food from the oil with a slotted spoon and drain well on kitchen paper. Deep-fried food is best served immediately, but if you need to keep it warm before serving, avoid covering the food or it will become soggy. Instead, put it in a single layer on a plate or baking sheet and keep it in a warm oven with the door ajar to allow air to circulate.

Stir-frying is an excellent, quick method of cooking food. It preserves valuable nutrients and retains the food's flavour, colour and texture. If you expect to do a lot of stir-frying, it's worth investing in a good wok, which is usually fairly inexpensive. The best modern woks are made from lightweight carbon steel, which is a good heat conductor and becomes non-stick when 'seasoned' properly and looked after. You can also deep-fry, steam and braise in a wok, so choose a good size that suits a wide-range of cooking methods, such as a 30–35cm/12–14in wok.

Preparation is key when stir-frying: make sure the vegetables are cut into uniform-sized pieces so they cook evenly, and measure all liquid ingredients before you begin. Choose an oil with a mild flavour and high smoking point, such as those recommended for deep-frying. Heat the wok over a high heat before you add the oil, then add the foods that take the longest to cook, such as onions and carrots. Leave other ingredients, such as leafy greens, bean sprouts and flavourings to the end to ensure that everything cooks evenly and reaches the right temperature. If you don't have a wok, a large, heavy-based frying pan is also suitable for stir-frying.

STEAM

Steaming allows foods to retain their texture, shape and flavour and can also revive dried ingredients by adding moisture. An important technique in Asian cooking, steaming is highly regarded for its relative ease and restorative qualities. Because foods are cooked in moist heat, rather than in fat or oil, it is one of the healthiest cooking techniques and is particularly good for delicate foods, vegetables, fruits, puddings, dumplings, grains and foods steamed in parcels.

There are two methods of steaming: direct and indirect. Direct steaming is the most common and involves placing a perforated basket over bubbling water and then covering it with a lid. The food cooks in the rising steam without coming into direct contact with the liquid. The steam must be able to circulate freely during cooking, so avoid overfilling the steamer basket or the food close to the lid will discolour and become soggy as the condensation that forms on the lid drips on to it. Half-full is ideal. Tiered bamboo steamers, found in Asian food shops, are specially designed for this purpose and can be placed over a wok. Vegetables, dumplings and other parcels are usually cooked by this form of steaming.

The indirect method of steaming is used for cooking steamed sweet and savoury puddings as well as rice. The sealed pudding basin is placed on a trivet or upturned saucer in a large pan, then enough boiling water is added to come halfway up the sides of the basin. This method tends to be quite slow since it takes a while for the heat to reach the centre of the basin, but it does give a light, open texture to a pudding. Two points to remember when steaming a pudding: avoid lifting the lid off the pan during the first 30 minutes because the drop in temperature may make the pudding sink. Also, keep an eye on water levels and occasionally top up with more boiling water, if necessary.

SIMMER

Simmering is the technique used to cook food in gently bubbling liquid, be it water, stock, wine or juice. It allows the flavours of the ingredients to merge and enhance each other, while still retaining their individual character.

Poaching is a perfect method for cooking certain fruits, vegetables and eggs. Poaching is normally done at a lower temperature than simmering: submerge the food in liquid and cook over a low heat so that the liquid barely trembles. It's great for slightly under-ripe fruit—in fact, avoid using very ripe fruit, which will disintegrate during cooking. Vegetables such as fennel, carrots, potatoes, courgettes and leeks also poach well in stock and make a lovely light stew or soup.

Poaching softens and sweetens fruit and is particularly suited to cherries, pears, peaches, nectarines and apricots. Submerge the fruit in a sugar syrup, wine or fruit juice, which can be flavoured with spices, such as cinnamon, ginger, cardamom or vanilla. If the fruit is likely to discolour, add a splash of lemon juice to prevent this.

To poach an egg, first crack it into a cup, then lower it into a sauté pan or small saucepan filled with about 5cm/2in of barely simmering water. (Some recommend swirling the water first to make a whirlpool, which encourages the egg to form a neat round.) Raise the heat slightly so that the water is gently bubbling and cook for 2–3 minutes until the white is set but the yolk remains runny. Remove the egg from the water with a slotted spoon and allow it to drain slightly, then serve warm.

Stewing is similar to poaching but uses less liquid. It is suitable for most fruits, transforming items such as apples, rhubarb, apricots and plums, for example, into a thick sauce or compôte. The fruit can then be passed through a sieve to make a purée or coulis.

Both poaching and stewing are particularly useful if you a have a glut of fruit you want to preserve, either as whole fruit, a thick compôte or jam for future use. Stewing is also the ideal method for cooking hearty winter fare, such as savoury stews, casseroles and soups. Some curries also benefit from stewing over a low, gentle heat, increasing the heat of the chilli and helping to meld the complex individual flavours of the spices. The beauty of this cooking technique is that dishes can be fully (or partially) cooked ahead of time and then reheated — remarkably often tasting better with time since the flavours are slowly and gently coaxed out.

Braising involves slow-cooking food that is half-submerged in liquid. The food is cooked in a covered pan for an extended time and absorbs most of the cooking liquid, producing a tender result. Leftover liquid can be used as a sauce.

Finally, boiling is vigorous and fast, with the heat set at a high temperature. When cooking pasta or noodles, it's important to keep them at a rolling boil to prevent the strands sticking together. Similarly, dense vegetables, such as potatoes and other root vegetables, often require boiling to soften them. Eggs, on the other hand, should not be boiled hard but simmered gently in just-bubbling water as vigorous boiling can crack the shells, toughen the whites and discolour the egg yolks.

Some of the recipes call for a vegetable to be blanched. This involves partially cooking it by boiling, then refreshing it under cold running water to stop the cooking process. It can then be cooked to completion just before serving.

BAKE

There is nothing more appealing than the intoxicating aroma of freshly baked bread. More than any other cooking technique, baking tells you when a food is ready by filling the kitchen with wonderful aromas.

The terms 'bake' and 'roast' are often used interchangeably, and there's really no hard and fast rule that distinguishes them. In both cases, food is cooked in the dry heat of an oven at temperatures usually above 150°C/300°F/gas 2. Rather loosely, 'baking' tends to be used to refer to breads, cakes, biscuits, pastries and pies. But then there are baked potatoes, fruit, stews, gratins and pasta dishes. 'Roasting' usually involves the use of fat to encourage a crisp or golden exterior and moist interior and is usually used to refer to savoury foods — although, again, there are many exceptions to this generalization.

Successful baking demands certain practices. Firstly, the oven needs to be preheated. This allows the food to start cooking at the correct temperature as soon as it is put in the oven, which is key. If you have a fan oven, check the manufacturer's recommendations for how to adjust baking times accordingly. Next, make sure you use the right size tin or baking dish, otherwise the cooking time and texture of the food may be affected. For some dishes, such as casseroles and gratins, this may not be crucial, but cakes and other delicate baked foods certainly require accuracy.

It's worth investing in good quality, heavy-duty trays and tins, too. They will last longer, conduct heat evenly and do not warp at high temperatures.

Fruit is great for baking and can be used in savoury dishes as well as sweet ones. The heat of the oven softens the cells of the fruit and intensifies its flavour by drying it slightly. Fruit can also be dry roasted to preserve it as well as to intensify its sweetness. This requires a low temperature and can take some time to extract the moisture from the fruit. Tomatoes also work well cooked in this way, and it's a great method for preserving a summer glut.

It's important when baking/roasting fruit and vegetables that they fit comfortably in an even layer in the tin, without overcrowding, to ensure they become golden and slightly caramelized, rather than cooking in their own moisture. Piling them on top of each other will trap in steam and cause them to become soggy instead of golden. If the baking tray is crowded, use two trays instead of one and swap their positions in the oven halfway through cooking. Foods with a high moisture content, such as tomatoes, courgettes, aubergines and garlic, will need more space than relatively dry foods, such as potatoes and root vegetables.

Vegetables and fruit can also be baked 'en papillote', or in a parcel, which seals in juices and helps to retain the nuances of any added flavourings.

PULSES, RICE AND SPROUTS
Here are some basic instructions for cooking dried pulses and rice, and for sprouting your own pulses or seeds.

PULSES
Pulses make an invaluable contribution to a meat-free diet and are versatile and nutritious. The recipes in this book call for 'cooked' beans, which can either be cooked from scratch or tinned. The former need a little advanced preparation but are more economical and taste better. There is much debate as to whether soaking dried beans before cooking is necessary. Lentils do not need soaking, but soaking certainly reduces the cooking time for other beans, including split peas, and can enhance their flavour because it starts the germination process.

Begin by rinsing the dried beans, then soak them in cold water for at least 4 hours or overnight if more convenient (soaking them for more than 4 hours has little influence on the cooking time). Drain and rinse the beans, then put them in a saucepan and cover with 2.5cm/1in cold water. Bring to the boil and boil rapidly for 10 minutes, then reduce the heat and simmer the beans, partially covered, until tender, about 45 minutes – 1 hour and 30 minutes, depending on the bean.

If you are short of time, the long soaking process can be speeded up: first cook the dried beans in boiling water for 2 minutes, then remove the pan from the heat, cover and leave to stand for about 2 hours. Drain, rinse and cover with fresh cold water before cooking, as described above.

Avoid adding salt or any acidic ingredients to the beans during cooking as this will prevent them from softening. Some cooks add bicarbonate of soda to the water to help soften the pulses, but this can reduce their nutritional value.

Dried pulses roughly double in weight and volume when cooked, so bear this in mind when following the recipes. All of the recipes call for 'cooked' beans, so if you are using dried beans, reduce the quantity called for by half and prepare as above. A drained 425g/15oz tin is roughly the equivalent of 150g/5½oz/¾ cup dried beans. If using tinned beans, rinse and drain them before use.

RICE

There are many methods of cooking rice, depending on personal preference and the type of rice being used, but the classic method for cooking boiled rice with fluffy, separate grains is the absorption method.

Use a long-grain white rice, such as basmati, and rinse the rice in several changes of water until it runs clear. Put the rice in a heavy-based saucepan and cover with about 1½ times the quantity of water or stock (it should be covered by about 1cm/½in fluid). Bring to the boil, uncovered, then turn the heat down to its lowest setting, cover with a lid, and simmer for about 10 minutes or until the water is absorbed. Remove the pan from the heat and leave to stand, covered, for 10 minutes, then fluff up the grains of rice with a fork to separate.

SPROUTING PULSES AND SEEDS

Sprouted beans are incredibly nutritious and add flavour and crunch to a dish. To grow your own, soak a good handful of dried pulses or seeds, such as mung beans, lentils or alfalfa, in lukewarm water overnight. Drain well, then transfer to a clean, sterilized jar. Cover the jar with a small piece of muslin and secure with a rubber band, then leave to stand in a warm, light place. Rinse, in the jar, twice a day under cold running water, draining well each time. The sprouts will be ready in 3–5 days. Transfer to an airtight container and store for up to 5 days in the fridge.

INGREDIENTS

Some recipes in this book use ingredients that you may be unfamiliar with or have heard of but not used. Here is a brief list of some of the more unusual.

BARBERRIES – These small, dark red dried berries have a sharp, sour flavour and are popular in Middle Eastern cuisine. They're available in Middle Eastern shops.

CHICKPEA FLOUR – Also known as gram flour or besan, this pale yellow flour is commonly used in Indian cooking. It gives a distinct flavour and texture to foods.

CHINESE BLACK BEANS – These fermented, salted black soya beans are available canned, in packets or dried at good Asian speciality shops. They need to be rinsed before use, and dried beans must be soaked in hot water for 20 minutes and rinsed well before use. They become very soft after soaking and can be used whole or ground to a paste as a substitute for bottled black bean sauce.

CHIPOTLE PASTE – A spicy paste made from smoked dried jalapeño peppers that is popular in Mexican cooking. Also look for dried chipotle chillies, which can be used dried in stews or soaked in hot water until softened and ground into a paste.

CURRY LEAVES – These small pointed leaves have a spicy flavour and often feature in Indian cooking. They can be frozen – use straight from the freezer – or dried.

ENOKI MUSHROOMS – Native to Japan, these long-stemmed mushrooms grow in clumps and have tiny white caps.

HARISSA – A chilli paste made with piri piri chillies, spices and tomatoes.

KABOCHA SQUASH – This Japanese winter squash has a dark green skin and vibrant, sweet orange flesh.

KECAP MANIS – This dark, thick, sweet soy sauce used in Indonesian and Malaysian cooking is now widely available, but if you can't find it substitute with dark soy sauce sweetened with a little sugar.

MIRIN – This sweet rice wine is used mainly in Japanese cooking in sauces, marinades and dressings.

MISO – A paste made from fermented soya beans, varying in colour from white and yellow to brown and red; generally, the lighter the colour, the milder the flavour.

MOOLI – A large, white root vegetable with a radishy flavour. Also known as daikon.

NORI – Seaweed that is formed into paper-like sheets, then dried. It is used as a wrapping for sushi or sold in flakes for sprinkling over dishes.

POMEGRANATE MOLASSES – A thick, dark, tangy syrup from the Middle East. It can be used in marinades and dressings or mixed with water to make a drink.

PRESERVED LEMONS – Popular in Moroccan cooking, these lemons are preserved in a salty brine, sometimes with added herbs and spices. They can be used in tagines and stews or finely chopped in salads and dressings.

QUINOA – This protein-rich, gluten-free grain has a mild, slightly bitter flavour.

RAMEN NOODLES – These Japanese noodles, made from wheat flour and egg, are often served in a broth of the same name.

RAS-EL-HANOUT – A popular North African blend of herbs and spices that is traditionally used in tagines. Some varieties contain as many as fifty ingredients.

RAW CACAO – Also known as raw chocolate, this is an antioxidant-rich, relatively unprocessed alternative to regular chocolate. Available in nibs and powder form.

RICE PAPER WRAPPERS – Dried, fragile rounds of paper-thin rice paper. These need to be soaked briefly in just-boiled water before use.

SHAOXING WINE – A Chinese fermented rice wine with a slightly sweet taste, reminiscent of dry sherry.

SOBA NOODLES – Made from buckwheat flour or a mixture of wheat and buckwheat, these Japanese noodles are popular served warm or cold.

SUMAC – A sour, slightly astringent, reddish-brown spice that comes from the dried berries of a bush that grows in the Mediterranean and the Middle East.

TAMARIND – A large, brown bean-like pod commonly sold as a paste, a block of compressed pulp (often with seeds) or puréed. It adds a sweet-sour flavour to Asian, Middle Eastern and Caribbean dishes.

TEMPEH – Made by fermenting soya beans with a cultured starter, rather like cheese-making, tempeh has a nutty, savoury flavour and firm texture.

TOGARASHI (SHICHIMI) – A Japanese spice blend made with ground chillies, orange peel, ground sansho, sesame seeds, poppy seeds, hemp seeds and nori.

TOFU – Made from ground soya beans, tofu is available in various textures, from firm, which holds its shape during cooking, to silken, which is very soft, smooth and creamy. Abura-age is a deep-fried golden tofu pocket that can be stuffed.

UME PLUM SEASONING – A tart, tangy seasoning made from the juices left over from the pickling of Japanese ume plums.

VEGETARIAN FISH SAUCE – Usually a combination of soya beans, salt, sugar, chilli and citric acid. Found in Thai and Vietnamese food shops.

WAKAME – This curly-leaf, brown seaweed is sold dried. After rehydrating, it has a soft texture and mild vegetable flavour.

WASABI – A pungent condiment made from Japanese horseradish.

Fresh and vibrant, these creative recipes show how easy it is to coax the best out of uncooked ingredients. They rely on techniques such as soaking, marinating, blending or slicing foods into paper-thin, translucent slivers and elegant 'noodles' to create a tantalizing combination of flavours, textures and colours.

RAW

Beetroot Carpaccio with Goat's Cheese and Orange–Balsamic Vinaigrette, page 24

VIETNAMESE RICE PAPER ROLLS WITH PEANUT NUOC CHAM

Nuoc cham is the classic accompaniment to most savoury snacks and starters in Vietnam. This dipping sauce is traditionally a mix of hot, sweet, sour and salty flavours and enlivens whatever it is served with, such as these delicious vegetable-filled rice paper rolls.

SERVES 4–6

6 spring onions, shredded
1 yellow pepper, deseeded and cut into thin strips
1 carrot, cut into matchsticks
75g/2 ½ oz/¾ cup finely shredded Chinese leaves
2 tbsp peeled and finely chopped ginger
2 garlic cloves, crushed
2 handfuls of bean sprouts
2 tbsp sweet chilli sauce
2 tbsp light soy sauce
2 tsp sesame oil
24 medium rice paper wrappers
4 long chives
110g/3 ¾ oz enoki mushrooms, trimmed and split into 4 or 6 bundles

NUOC CHAM DIPPING SAUCE
½ small cucumber, deseeded and diced
1 garlic clove, crushed
2 tsp palm sugar or soft light brown sugar
1 bird's eye chilli, finely chopped
2 tbsp vegetarian fish sauce
juice of 1 lime
2 tbsp light soy sauce
1 tbsp roasted peanuts, coarsely chopped

1 Put the spring onions, yellow pepper, carrot, Chinese leaves, ginger, garlic and bean sprouts in a large mixing bowl. In a small bowl, mix together the chilli sauce, soy sauce and sesame oil. Pour the mixture over the vegetables and toss well.

2 Fill a heatproof bowl with just-boiled water. Put 2 rice paper wrappers on top of one another (you will need 2 per roll as they are very fragile) and soak in the water for 20 seconds or until they are pliable and opaque. Use a spatula to carefully remove the wrappers from the water, drain for a second and place flat on a plate. Pat dry with kitchen towel, then spread a spoonful of the vegetable mixture vertically down the centre of the top wrapper. Fold the bottom edge over to enclose the filling and make a base, then roll the wrapper over the filling from left to right, leaving the top open. Repeat with the remaining wrappers and filling to make 12 rolls in total.

3 Tie 1 chive around each bundle of enoki mushrooms.

4 Mix together all of the ingredients for the nuoc cham dipping sauce and divide it into four small bowls.

5 Serve 2 or 3 rice paper rolls per person, accompanied by the dipping sauce and an enoki bundle.

TRIO OF CASHEW NUT CHEESES

Soaked and blended cashews make a remarkably creamy soft 'cheese'. Garlic and lemon, herbs and nuts are just a few of the many flavourings you can use.

SERVES 4
300g/10½ oz/2 cups cashew nuts
½ tsp salt
1 garlic clove, crushed
1 tbsp lemon juice
a large pinch of smoked paprika
5 tbsp shelled pistachios, finely chopped
5 tbsp chopped mixed herbs, such as thyme, oregano and chives
freshly ground black pepper
savoury biscuits, to serve

1 Put the cashews in a bowl, cover with warm water and leave to soak for at least 2 hours, then drain and transfer the cashews to a food processor or blender. Add 185ml/6fl oz/¾ cup water and blend into a coarse paste. (For a softer 'cheese', add a little more water and blend into a coarse purée.) Add the salt and season with pepper.

2 Divide the nut cheese into 3 equal portions. Stir the garlic, lemon juice and paprika into 1 portion and spoon it into a ramekin. Put the chopped pistachios on a plate. Using your hands, divide another portion of the nut cheese into teaspoon-sized balls, then roll each ball in the pistachios until evenly coated. Roll the last portion of the nut cheese into a log and roll it in the herbs to coat. Serve the flavoured nut cheeses with biscuits.

NECTARINE, BOCCONCINI AND BASIL SALAD WITH VERJUICE DRESSING

Verjuice is the unfermented juice of unripe wine grapes and makes a refreshing alternative to lemon juice or wine vinegar in salad dressings. If you can't get hold of bocconcini (baby mozzarella cheese), you can use a single ball of mozzarella cheese sliced into rounds. Serve with crusty bread.

SERVES 4
3 tbsp pine nuts
3 nectarines, halved, stoned and sliced
300g/10½ oz bocconcini (baby mozzarella cheese), drained
1 handful of basil leaves, roughly torn

VERJUICE DRESSING
3 tbsp olive oil
1 tbsp verjuice
salt and freshly ground black pepper

1 Toast the pine nuts in a dry frying pan and over a medium heat for 3–4 minutes, stirring occasionally, until lightly browned. Watch carefully so they do not burn. Remove from the heat and set aside.

2 In a small bowl, mix together all of the ingredients for the dressing and season with salt and pepper.

3 Arrange the nectarine slices in a shallow dish and top with the bocconcini. Sprinkle with the basil leaves and drizzle with the dressing. Top with the pine nuts and serve.

BEETROOT CARPACCIO WITH GOAT'S CHEESE AND ORANGE–BALSAMIC VINAIGRETTE

SERVES 4

2 tbsp orange juice
½ tsp balsamic vinegar
4 tbsp olive oil
¼ tsp salt
1 beetroot, peeled
½ tsp lemon juice
2 large handfuls of mixed leaves,
    such as watercress and rocket
100g/3½ oz goat's cheese, thinly
    sliced into rounds
2 tbsp pumpkin seeds
freshly ground black pepper

1 Put the orange juice, vinegar, oil and salt in a bowl and whisk or blend with an immersion blender until well mixed and thickened, then set aside.

2 Using a very sharp knife or a mandolin, cut the beetroot into paper-thin rounds. Put them in a bowl with the lemon juice and add just enough cold water to cover.

3 Divide the mixed leaves on to four plates, then top with the drained beetroot and goat's cheese, alternating the two in a horizontal row across the mixed leaves. Sprinkle with the pumpkin seeds and drizzle with the vinaigrette, then season with black pepper and serve.

BLACK OLIVE TAPENADE, DOLCELATTE AND PINE NUT WRAPS

SERVES 4

3 tbsp pine nuts
4 large multi-seed tortillas
1 large handful of baby spinach
    leaves, tough stalks removed
1 small red pepper, deseeded and
    cut into thin strips
70g/2½ oz/heaped ½ cup creamy
    dolcelatte cheese, cut into small
    chunks with the rind removed
salt and freshly ground black pepper

TAPENADE

85g/3oz/¾ cup pitted black olives
1 garlic clove
2 tbsp extra-virgin olive oil
1 tbsp lemon juice
2 tbsp chopped flat-leaf parsley
    leaves

1 To make the tapenade, put the olives and garlic in a food processor and process until coarsely chopped. Add the olive oil and lemon juice and process again to obtain a coarse purée. Transfer to a bowl, season with salt and pepper, and stir in the parsley.

2 Toast the pine nuts in a dry frying pan over a medium heat for 3–4 minutes, stirring occasionally, until lightly browned. Remove the pine nuts from the pan, then put 2 of the tortillas in the pan and warm them over a medium-low heat, turning occasionally, for about 20 seconds. Repeat with the remaining tortillas.

3 Spread 1 tablespoon of the tapenade down the centre of each tortilla and top with the spinach, red pepper, Dolcelatte and pine nuts. Season with salt and pepper and roll up, tucking in the ends, then cut in half crossways on the diagonal and serve.

CHILLED ALMOND SOUP WITH FRUIT AND OLIVE KEBABS

A version of the classic Spanish *Ajo Blanco*, this chilled garlicky soup is served with a kebab of apple, olives and grapes for dunking. In Spain, the soup is traditionally served as a first course at Christmas lunch.

SERVES 4

4 thick slices of white bread, crusts removed
200g/7oz/1⅓ cups blanched almonds
3 garlic cloves, crushed
1 tsp salt
150ml/5fl oz/scant ⅔ cup extra-virgin olive oil
3 tbsp verjuice or white wine vinegar
1 green apple
1 tbsp lemon juice
16 green grapes
12 pitted green olives
ice cubes, to serve

1 Soak the bread in water for 10 minutes. Meanwhile, finely chop the almonds in a food processor or blender. Add the garlic, salt, olive oil, verjuice and 250ml/9fl oz/1 cup water.

2 Squeeze the bread in your hands to remove as much water as possible, then add it to the food processor. Process until smooth and creamy, then add another 250ml/9fl oz/1 cup water and process again. Cover and chill the soup for at least 2 hours.

3 Just before serving, make the kebabs. Peel, core and cut the apple into bite-sized chunks, then toss in the lemon juice to prevent them from discolouring. Thread the apple chunks, 4 grapes and 3 olives on to each of four skewers. Ladle the soup into four bowls (if it is very thick, add a little more water first) and add a few ice cubes to each portion. Top with a kebab and serve immediately.

KOHLRABI, MANGO AND HERB NORI CONES

If making sushi sounds daunting, these filled nori cones are a great starting point because they don't require any fiddly rolling or special tools. The softness of the noodles is a wonderful contrast to the crisp texture and slight heat of the kohlrabi and the sweetness of the fresh mango.

SERVES 4

50g/1 ¾ oz vermicelli rice noodles
1 tbsp ume plum seasoning or rice
   vinegar
4 nori sheets, quartered
4 tsp wasabi paste
16 large basil leaves
½ mango, peeled, stoned and cut
   into strips
100g/3 ½ oz kohlrabi or turnip,
   peeled and cut into matchsticks
2 spring onions, sliced
leaves from a few sprigs of coriander

PLUM DIPPING SAUCE

4 tbsp plum sauce
2.5cm/1in piece of root ginger,
   peeled and cut into fine
   matchsticks

1 To make the dipping sauce, mix together the plum sauce, ginger and 4 tablespoons warm water in a small bowl, then set aside.

2 Put the noodles in a bowl and add enough boiling water to cover them. Stir to separate the noodles, then leave to stand, covered, for 5–7 minutes until softened. Drain the noodles and refresh under cold running water. Return the noodles to the bowl, add the ume plum seasoning and turn until coated.

3 To make the nori cones, smear a little wasabi diagonally down the centre of each nori square. Top with 1 large basil leaf, then with 1 tablespoon of noodles, leaving a little gap at the bottom of the nori to allow you to roll it up. Put 1 strip of mango, 4 sticks of kohlrabi, a little spring onion and a few coriander leaves on top of the noodles. Take the nori sheet in your hand and roll into a cone shape. Wet the edge of the nori and press to seal. Repeat to make 15 more cones. Serve with the dipping sauce.

VIETNAMESE TOFU AND MANGO SALAD CUPS

SERVES 4

250g/9oz firm smoked tofu

16 large Little Gem lettuce leaves

1 mango, peeled, stoned and cut into strips with a vegetable peeler

1 small cucumber, cut into thin, 2.5cm/1in long slices

1 small handful of mint leaves, chopped

1 small handful of coriander leaves, chopped

2 tbsp coarsely chopped roasted peanuts

salt

CHILLI & LIME DRESSING

2 tbsp vegetarian fish sauce

4 tbsp lime juice

1 red chilli, thinly sliced into rounds

1 small garlic clove, crushed

1 tsp caster sugar

1 To make the dressing, mix all of the ingredients together in a small serving bowl and set aside.

2 Pat the tofu dry with a piece of kitchen towel, then slice it into 1cm/½in slices.

3 Arrange the lettuce leaves on a plate. Divide the mango, cucumber and tofu on to the lettuce leaves, using each leaf as a 'cup'. Sprinkle with the mint and coriander leaves, then spoon a little dressing over each one. Top with the peanuts and serve.

AVOCADO AND BEETROOT SALAD WITH HORSERADISH DRESSING

SERVES 4

2 tbsp sunflower seeds

2 tbsp pumpkin seeds

1 avocado

200g/7oz mixed baby salad leaves

1 beetroot, peeled and coarsely grated

1 small handful of alfalfa and broccoli sprouts

HORSERADISH DRESSING

2 tbsp olive oil

1 tbsp lemon juice

1 tbsp cider vinegar

1 tbsp creamed horseradish

1 tbsp single cream

salt and freshly ground black pepper

1 Toast the seeds in a dry frying pan over a medium heat for 3–5 minutes, stirring occasionally, until slightly golden. Watch carefully so they do not burn. Remove from the heat and set aside.

2 To make the dressing, whisk together all of the ingredients with 1 tablespoon warm water, season with salt and pepper and set aside.

3 Cut the avocado in half, remove the stone and scoop out the flesh, then cut the flesh into small chunks.

4 Line a serving plate with the baby salad leaves and top with the beetroot, avocado and sprouts. Drizzle with the dressing and sprinkle the toasted seeds over the top just before serving.

MEXICAN GAZPACHO

Lime, coriander and tequila give this classic chilled soup a Mexican feel.
For the best flavour, use perfectly ripe tomatoes – take a sniff, they should
smell beautifully aromatic.

SERVES 4

2 slices of day-old bread, crusts
   removed
1kg/2lb 4oz tomatoes
1 cucumber, peeled, deseeded and
   chopped
1 red pepper, deseeded and chopped
1–2 jalapeño chillies, deseeded and
   finely chopped
2 garlic cloves
1 tbsp chopped oregano leaves
2 tbsp olive oil
1–2 tbsp tequila
juice of 2 limes
salt
ice cubes, to serve

AVOCADO SALSA

1 avocado
1 tsp lime juice
½ small red onion, finely chopped
4 tbsp cooked black beans
2 tbsp chopped coriander leaves

1 Soak the bread in 150ml/5fl oz/scant ⅔ cup cold water for
5 minutes. Meanwhile, put the tomatoes in a bowl, cover with
boiling water and leave to stand for 30 seconds, then drain. Peel,
deseed and chop the flesh.

2 Put half of the bread, tomatoes, cucumber, red pepper, chillies,
garlic, oregano, olive oil, tequila and lime juice in a food processor
or blender. Add 270ml/9½ fl oz/generous 1 cup cold water
and process until combined but still chunky. Transfer to a large
bowl and repeat with the rest of the ingredients. Combine the
two batches and season with salt to taste. Cover and chill for
2–3 hours.

3 Just before serving, make the avocado salsa. Cut the avocado in
half, remove the stone and scoop the flesh out, using a large spoon.
Cut the flesh into small cubes and put it in a bowl. Mix in the lime
juice, red onion, black beans and coriander leaves.

4 Ladle the soup into bowls, add the ice cubes and top with a large
spoonful of the salsa. Serve immediately.

NOODLES WITH VEGETABLE SPAGHETTI AND MISO DRESSING

The success of this vibrant salad relies on slicing the vegetables into fine shreds, or julienne, so their flavours blend and take on the nuances of the miso dressing.

SERVES 4
225g/8oz vermicelli rice noodles
1 tbsp sesame seeds
1 courgette
1 large carrot
100g/3½oz mooli, peeled
100g/3½oz red cabbage, finely
    shredded
5 spring onions, finely sliced
1 heaped tbsp nori flakes
1 handful of basil leaves, torn
1 handful of coriander leaves,
    chopped
1 small handful of radish sprouts
salt and freshly ground black pepper

MISO DRESSING
3 tbsp yellow miso paste
3 tbsp rice vinegar
2 tsp light soy sauce
3 tsp sesame oil
2 tbsp sunflower oil
1 tsp English mustard powder
2 tbsp peeled and very finely chopped
    root ginger

1 Put the noodles in a heatproof bowl and cover with just-boiled water. Stir to separate the noodles and leave to stand, covered, for 5 minutes or until tender. Drain, refresh under cold running water, return to the bowl and cover with cold water until ready to serve.

2 Meanwhile, toast the sesame seeds in a dry frying pan over a medium heat for 3–4 minutes, stirring occasionally, until slightly golden. Watch carefully so they do not burn. Remove from the heat and set aside.

3 Slice the courgette, carrot and mooli into long, thin strips or julienne using a mandolin, microplane or paring knife.

4 To make the dressing, mix together the miso and vinegar with 1 tablespoon hot water until smooth. Stir in the soy sauce, sesame and sunflower oils, mustard powder and ginger, then season with salt and pepper.

5 Drain the noodles and put them in a serving bowl. Add half of the dressing and, using your hands, turn until the noodles are coated. Add the courgette, carrot, mooli, cabbage, spring onions, nori and half of the basil and coriander leaves and toss well. Drizzle with the remaining dressing and serve immediately, topped with the remaining herbs, sesame seeds and radish sprouts.

STUFFED TOMATOES WITH CRUSHED BEANS, MOZZARELLA AND CHIMICHURRI

Chimichurri is an Argentinian herb and garlic sauce, rather like pesto with an edge — it adds a simple, vibrant oomph to a dish. I've used canned pulses here, but you could soak and cook dried ones, if you prefer. Burrata, often referred to as the rich cousin of mozzarella, is a great, creamy alternative cheese to try here.

SERVES 4

4 beefsteak tomatoes
400g/14oz tinned cannellini beans, drained and rinsed
2 tbsp extra-virgin olive oil, plus extra for drizzling
juice of 1 lemon
1 small red onion, diced
70g/2½oz/½ cup pitted black olives, coarsely chopped
175g/6oz mozzarella cheese, drained and torn into chunks
2 courgettes, trimmed
2 tbsp chopped mint leaves
salt and freshly ground black pepper

CHIMICHURRI

1 large handful of flat-leaf parsley leaves, finely chopped
2 large garlic cloves, crushed
125ml/4fl oz/½ cup olive oil, plus extra for drizzling
3 tbsp sherry vinegar or red wine vinegar
2 tsp dried oregano
1 tsp ground cumin
½ tsp dried chilli flakes
½ tsp salt
4 tbsp chopped coriander leaves

1 Cut off the top of each tomato and scoop out and discard the core and seeds. Put the tomatoes upside down on a plate and set aside to drain.

2 To make the chimichurri, mix together all of the ingredients in a bowl, then set aside.

3 Put the beans in a small mixing bowl and crush roughly with the back of a fork or a potato masher. Stir in the olive oil, lemon juice, red onion and olives, then season with salt and pepper.

4 Slice off a sliver from the base of each tomato to allow them to stand. Spoon the bean mixture into each tomato until filled nearly to the top. Divide the mozzarella over the top and spoon the chimichurri sauce over the cheese.

5 Using a mandolin or vegetable peeler, slice the courgettes into ribbons. Drizzle a little olive oil over the courgettes, then sprinkle with the mint and season lightly with salt and pepper. Serve the courgettes on top of the tomatoes or alongside.

FATTOUSH WITH LABNEH AND PRESERVED LEMON DRESSING

Labneh, a soft, creamy yogurt cheese, popular in the Middle East, is fun and easy to make at home – but you need to start it a full day ahead. It's well worth experimenting when making labneh. Try flavouring it with crushed garlic, chopped herbs or ground spices. For a quicker, softer cheese, reduce the draining time for the Greek yogurt to 6–8 hours. You could also double the labneh recipe and roll tablespoons of the cheese into balls – you should have about 15. Put them in a tall, sterilized glass jar, cover with olive oil and keep in the fridge for up to 1 week.

SERVES 4

1 large pitta bread
6 tomatoes, halved, deseeded and
    cut into bite-sized chunks
1 small cucumber, quartered
    lengthways, deseeded and cut
    into bite-sized chunks
1 large red pepper, quartered
    lengthways, deseeded and cut
    into bite-sized chunks
1 small red onion, thinly sliced into
    rings
4 tbsp chopped mint leaves
4 tbsp chopped flat-leaf parsley
    leaves
seeds from ½ pomegranate,
    separated (optional)

LABNEH
250g/9oz/1 cup Greek yogurt
½ tsp salt

PRESERVED LEMON DRESSING
1½ preserved lemons
5 tbsp extra-virgin olive oil
1 tbsp lemon juice
½ tsp ground sumac or ground
    cumin
salt and freshly ground black pepper

1 To make the labneh, line a strainer with a piece of muslin or cheesecloth and rest it over a medium mixing bowl. Mix together the yogurt and salt and spoon it into the cloth. Draw the edges of the muslin up and twist the top to make a bundle, then leave to drain in the fridge for about 24 hours, gently squeezing it occasionally to help the liquid to drain.

2 To make the dressing, cut the lemon rind away from the flesh. Discard the flesh and finely chop the rind. In a small bowl, mix together the olive oil and lemon juice, stir in the sumac and lemon rind and season with salt and pepper.

3 Slice around the edge of the pitta bread to open it up and toast it in a dry frying pan or under a grill for a few minutes until crisp. Leave to cool slightly, then break into bite-sized pieces.

4 Put the tomatoes, cucumber, red pepper, red onion, mint and parsley in a large, shallow bowl. Add the dressing and toss to combine. Sprinkle the pomegranate and pitta crisps over the top.

5 Remove the yogurt from the cloth – it should now look like a semi-soft cheese. Crumble it into chunks and arrange on top of the salad, then serve.

SAVOURY CHEESECAKE WITH RED PEPPER AND CORIANDER RELISH

The finely chopped red peppers, chillies and red onion relish here add colour, crunch and plenty of zingy flavour, which is in sharp contrast to the mild creaminess of the savoury cheesecake.

SERVES 4–6

150g/5½oz/ 1 cup chopped roasted hazelnuts

50g/1¾oz/⅓ cup cashew nuts

12 coarse oatcakes, broken

50g/1¾oz butter, melted

300g/10½oz/heaped 1¼ cups cream cheese

100g/3½oz/scant ½ cup ricotta cheese

100g/3½oz/scant ¾ cup feta cheese, finely chopped

2 eggs, separated

2 tsp paprika

salt and freshly ground black pepper

RED PEPPER AND CORIANDER RELISH

2 red peppers, deseeded and diced

2 green chillies, deseeded and diced

1 small red onion, diced

1 large handful of coriander, coarsely chopped

juice of 1 lime

1 Put the hazelnuts and cashews in a food processor and pulse until finely ground. Add the oatcakes and process again to form fine crumbs. Transfer the mixture to a bowl, season with salt and pepper and add the melted butter. Stir until combined, then press into the base of a 20cm/8in loose-bottom, non-stick flan tin (you can also use individual tins if desired). Chill for 30 minutes.

2 In a large bowl, blend together the cream cheese, ricotta, feta, egg yolks and half of the paprika and season with salt and pepper. In a clean bowl, whisk the egg whites until they form soft peaks, then gently fold them into the cheese mixture. Spoon the mixture into the tin and smooth the surface. Cover and chill for about 2 hours until firm.

3 Mix together all of the ingredients for the relish and season with salt.

4 Remove the cheesecake from the tin, leaving the base, then dust with the remaining paprika. Cut into slices and serve topped with a good spoonful of the relish.

APPLE, FENNEL AND WALNUT SALAD

A mandolin may not be a must-have piece of kitchen equipment, but it makes slicing vegetables into paper-thin slivers incredibly easy.

SERVES 4

30g/1oz/¼ cup walnut halves
2 tbsp extra-virgin olive oil
2 tbsp lemon juice
1 tsp wholegrain mustard
4 tbsp soured cream
150g/5½ oz red cabbage, shredded
1 small fennel bulb, thinly sliced lengthways
1 green apple, thinly sliced horizontally, seeds discarded
2 tbsp chopped flat-leaf parsley leaves
salt and freshly ground black pepper

1 Preheat the oven to 180°C/350°F/gas 4. Put the walnuts on a baking sheet and bake for 6–8 minutes until lightly toasted, then set aside to cool.
2 Meanwhile, in a small bowl, whisk together the olive oil and lemon juice, then mix in the mustard and soured cream. Season with salt and pepper and set aside.
3 Put the cabbage, fennel, apple and parsley in a mixing bowl, add the dressing and toss well. Top with the walnuts and serve immediately.

TURNIP, RADISH AND DILL SALAD WITH MUSTARD DRESSING

This crunchy winter salad proves just how delicious most root vegetables are when served raw – just as good, if not better, than when cooked.

SERVES 4

150g/5½ oz turnips, peeled
10 radishes, trimmed
150g/5½ oz celeriac, peeled and coarsely grated
2 tbsp small capers, drained and rinsed
1 tbsp chopped dill

MUSTARD DRESSING

5 tbsp extra-virgin olive oil
2 tbsp cider vinegar
2 tsp Dijon mustard
1 large garlic clove, peeled and halved
salt and freshly ground black pepper

1 Whisk together all of the ingredients for the dressing and season with salt and pepper.
2 Slice the turnips and radishes into thin rounds using a mandolin or sharp knife. Put them in a serving bowl, add the celeriac and toss to combine. Sprinkle the capers on top.
3 Remove and discard the garlic from the dressing, then drizzle it over the salad. Sprinkle with the dill before serving.

SPROUTED BEAN, ROCKET AND PEA SHOOT SALAD

The nutritional value of pulses increases significantly when sprouted, providing around 60 per cent more vitamin C. Most supermarkets carry a variety of sprouts, so experiment to find the ones you like best. They are also easy to grow at home in a sprouter, if you have one, or even in a jam jar (see page 15).

SERVES 4
4 tbsp extra-virgin olive oil
2 tbsp lemon juice
1 tsp Dijon mustard
3 tbsp chopped garlic chives
   or chives
3 tbsp chopped basil leaves
100g/3½oz rocket leaves
100g/3½oz pea shoots
50g/1¾oz sugar snap peas,
   trimmed and thinly sliced
1 small handful of mixed sprouted
   beans
1 small red onion, thinly sliced
salt and freshly ground black pepper

1 To make the dressing, whisk together the olive oil, lemon juice and mustard in a small bowl. Stir in the chives and basil and season with salt and pepper.
2 Put the rocket, pea shoots and sugar snap peas in a bowl and toss to combine. Top with the sprouted beans and red onion. Spoon the dressing over the salad and serve immediately.

CRUNCHY ORIENTAL SLAW

SERVES 4
85g/3oz/¾ cup shredded white
   cabbage
85g/3oz/¾ cup shredded red
   cabbage
2 carrots, grated
4 spring onions, finely sliced
3 tbsp chopped mint leaves
3 tbsp shredded basil leaves

SESAME AND GINGER DRESSING
2.5cm/1in piece of root ginger,
   peeled and grated
2 tbsp olive oil
4 tsp toasted sesame oil
2 tbsp rice vinegar
salt and freshly ground black pepper

1 To make the dressing, squeeze the ginger in one hand to extract the juice into a bowl. Whisk in the remaining ingredients and season with salt and pepper.
2 Put the white and red cabbage, carrots, spring onions, mint and basil in a bowl. Add the dressing and toss to coat. This slaw is at its best served at room temperature.

CARAMEL, CHOCOLATE AND MAPLE SEMIFREDDO

Gloriously simple, this creamy, maple-sweetened indulgence is decorated with frozen grapes. These may sound unusual, but they take on a whole new character when frozen – almost like mini fruit lollies – and an attractive icy bloom.

SERVES 8–10

3 eggs, separated

125g/4½ oz/heaped ½ cup caster sugar

2 tbsp maple syrup

300ml/10½ fl oz/scant 1¼ cups double cream

100g/3½ oz milk chocolate with toffee or caramel pieces, finely chopped

8–10 sprigs of seedless black grapes, to serve

1 Line the base and sides of a 900g/2lb loaf tin with a double layer of cling film, leaving enough excess hanging over the edges to completely cover the semifreddo. In a large bowl, whisk the eggs yolks, caster sugar and maple syrup until pale and light. In another bowl, whip the cream until it forms soft peaks. In a third clean bowl, whisk the egg whites until they form firm peaks. Gently fold the whipped cream into the egg yolk mixture, then gradually fold in the egg whites to make a light, fluffy mixture.

2 Sprinkle a third of the chocolate into the base of the tin. Pour half of the cream mixture over the chocolate, followed by another third of the chocolate. Pour in the remaining cream mixture and sprinkle the rest of the chocolate over the top in an even layer. Cover with the excess cling film and freeze for 4–6 hours or until solid.

3 Wash the grapes without removing them from the vine (you want 1 sprig per person) and put them on a baking tray. Freeze for 1–2 hours or until frozen.

4 Remove the grapes and semifreddo from the freezer 10 minutes ahead of serving time. Unpeel the top of the cling film, then turn the semifreddo out on to a serving plate. Peel away the rest of the cling film and cut the semifreddo into slices. Top with the frozen grapes and serve immediately.

VANILLA CHEESECAKES WITH BLACKBERRIES IN CASSIS

SERVES 4

100g/3½oz/scant 1 cup
  blackberries

2 tbsp crème de cassis liqueur

225g/8oz/1 cup cream cheese

40g/1½oz/⅓ cup icing sugar

2 tsp vanilla extract

4 tbsp double cream

HAZELNUT BASE

sunflower oil, for greasing

60g/2¼oz/½ cup roasted chopped
  hazelnuts

25g/1oz/½ cup jumbo oats

2 tsp virgin coconut oil, melted if
  hard

1 tbsp agave syrup or maple syrup

1 Put the blackberries and cassis in a bowl and leave to steep for at least 30 minutes.

2 Meanwhile, lightly grease four 6cm/2½in presentation rings and arrange them on a small baking sheet. In a food processor, grind the nuts and oats until the consistency of coarse breadcrumbs. Add the coconut oil and agave syrup and pulse until combined. Divide the mixture into the rings and press down with the back of a teaspoon to make a firm, level base. Chill while you make the topping.

3 Beat together the cream cheese, icing sugar, vanilla extract and double cream until thickened. Spoon the mixture over the cheesecake bases and level the tops. Chill for 1 hour until firm.

4 To serve, carefully run a knife around the inside of the rings to loosen the cheesecakes on to serving plates. Decorate the top of each cheesecake with the blackberries and spoon a little of the cassis over the top, then serve.

RAW APRICOT AND ALMOND PANFORTE

Praised as one of nature's superfoods, raw cacao, or raw chocolate, is nutritionally potent. Combining it with nuts, seeds and dried fruit in this recipe creates a delicious, healthy treat.

MAKES 8 BARS

25g/1oz/¼ cup coarsely chopped
  blanched almonds

25g/1oz/¼ cup coarsely chopped
  toasted hazelnuts

50g/1¾oz/½ cup jumbo oats

2 tbsp pumpkin seeds

2 tbsp sunflower seeds

150g/5½oz/1 cup ready-to-eat
  unsulphured dried apricots,
  coarsely chopped

100g/3½oz/¾ cup raisins

5 tbsp freshly squeezed orange juice

2 tbsp raw cacao powder

2 tbsp raw cacao nibs

1 Put the almonds, hazelnuts, oats, pumpkin and sunflower seeds in a food processor and process until finely chopped. Transfer the mixture into a mixing bowl.

2 Put the apricots, raisins and orange juice in the food processor and purée to a smooth, thick paste; you may need to occasionally scrape the fruit mixture from the side of the food processor bowl to get the right consistency. Scrape the fruit purée into the bowl with the nut mixture, add the cacao powder and nibs and mix well.

3 Line a 25 x 18cm/10 x 7in baking tin with baking paper or cling film. Transfer the nut and fruit mixture to the tin and, using a palette knife, smooth into an even layer about 1cm/½in thick. Chill for 1 hour, then cut into 8 bars and serve.

WATERMELON AND VODKA CRUSH WITH POMEGRANATE

Vibrant and refreshing, this 'grown-up' granita is a great simple dinner party dessert. For a dramatic, modern look, freeze it in cone-shaped ice cream moulds or a cone made from baking paper.

SERVES 4 OR 6

1.5kg/3lb 5oz watermelon
70g/2½ oz/scant ⅓ cup caster sugar
5 tbsp vodka
1 tbsp lemon juice
finely shredded zest of ½ lime
pomegranate seeds, to serve

1 Cut the watermelon into wedges, then cut away the black seeds and skin. Cut the flesh into chunks and purée in a blender. Press the purée through a sieve into a bowl, then add the sugar and stir until it has dissolved. Stir in the vodka and lemon juice.

2 Pour into 4 or 6 cone-shaped ice cream moulds or a 1l/35fl oz/ 4-cup freezer-proof container with a lid. Cover the cones with cling film or the container with its lid, and freeze for 3–4 hours until frozen.

3 Remove from the freezer about 15 minutes before serving to soften slightly, then gently slip the ices out of the moulds, if using, or scrape the top with a fork and divide the ice crystals into glasses. Sprinkle with the lime zest and pomegranate seeds and serve immediately.

MANGO KULFI WITH FRESH BERRIES

SERVES 8

1 large ripe mango, peeled and pitted
1 tsp vanilla extract
400ml/14fl oz/scant 1¾ cups evaporated milk
60ml/2fl oz/¼ cup condensed milk
sunflower oil, for greasing
2 tbsp chopped unsalted pistachios
silver leaf, to decorate (optional)
250g/9oz/heaped 2 cups mixed summer berries, such a blackberries, redcurrants, raspberries and strawberries

1 Put the mango, vanilla extract, evaporated milk and condensed milk in a food processor or blender and blend until smooth and creamy.

2 Lightly oil eight 150ml/5fl oz/scant ⅔ cup dariole or pudding moulds or a 1l/35fl oz/4-cup freezer-proof container with a lid. Divide the kulfi mixture into the moulds or container. Cover the moulds with cling film or the container with its lid and freeze for 1 hour, then stir with a fork to break up any ice crystals. Smooth the top and return to the freezer. Freeze for another 3 hours or until frozen solid.

3 To remove the kulfi from the moulds, take them out of the freezer 15 minutes before serving. Run a knife around the side of each one, then turn upside down and give the mould a little shake to release the kulfi on to a serving plate. You can also put the moulds in a bowl of hot water for a few seconds to help release the kulfi.

4 Sprinkle the pistachios over the tops and decorate with a few flakes of silver leaf, if using. Serve immediately with the mixed berries.

ORANGE-DRENCHED DATE AND RAW CHOCOLATE TRUFFLES

MAKES 18
50g/1¾ oz/⅓ cup blanched almonds
50g/1¾ oz/⅓ cup cashew nuts
100g/3½ oz/heaped 1 cup ready-to-eat dried pitted dates, coarsely chopped
3 tbsp orange juice
grated zest of 1 orange
1 tbsp agave syrup or honey
3 tbsp raw cacao powder, plus extra for coating
seeds from 2–3 green cardamom pods
55g/2oz/heaped ½ cup desiccated coconut, for coating

1 Put the almonds and cashews in a food processor and process until ground, then transfer to a mixing bowl. Put the dates in the food processor and process to a paste. You may have to stop occasionally to scrape the dates from the side of the food processor bowl. Put the date paste in the bowl with the nuts and add the orange juice and zest, agave syrup and raw cacao powder.
2 Using a mortar and pestle, grind the cardamom seeds, then add them to the bowl. Stir until combined into a thick paste.
3 Coat a plate with extra raw cacao powder. Shape 1 tablespoon of the date and nut mixture into a ball and roll it in the cacao. Repeat to make 9 cacao-coated truffles in total.
4 Coat a second plate with desiccated coconut. Follow the same method in step 3 to make 9 more truffles, this time rolling them in the coconut. Chill the truffles until ready to eat.

SHRIKHAND WITH BLUEBERRIES

Sweet, creamy and indulgent, this classic Indian dessert is made from strained yogurt and has a golden colour thanks to the addition of saffron. For a quicker version, use Greek yogurt instead of plain and omit the draining stage. Simply mix the Greek yogurt with the cream and continue from step 2.

SERVES 4
500ml/17fl oz/2 cups natural yogurt
8 saffron strands
2 tbsp warm milk
100ml/3½ fl oz/scant ½ cup double cream
4 tbsp caster sugar
1 vanilla pod, split and seeds scraped out
1 tsp cinnamon
40g/1½ oz dark chocolate
½ tsp freshly ground nutmeg
150g/5½ oz/1¼ cups blueberries

1 Line a sieve with a piece of muslin or cheesecloth and rest it over a bowl. Add the yogurt, draw the edges of the muslin up and twist the top to make a bundle. Leave to drain for 3 hours (or overnight if you have time) to drain the whey, gently squeezing it occasionally to help it drain.
2 Soak the saffron in the warm milk for 15 minutes. Put the drained yogurt, cream and caster sugar in a mixing bowl and whisk until thickened. Stir in the vanilla seeds, cinnamon and saffron mixture and divide into four small glasses or bowls. Chill for 30 minutes.
3 Meanwhile, cut the chocolate into curls using a vegetable peeler. Sprinkle the chocolate and nutmeg over the shrikhand and serve with the blueberries.

STRAWBERRY AND MARSALA SYLLABUBS

Marsala wine is the perfect match for strawberries and cream. The cream shouldn't be over-beaten but whisked until it forms soft, billowy peaks.

SERVES 4

500g/1lb 2oz strawberries, hulled

4 tsp icing sugar

2 tbsp caster sugar

3 tbsp Marsala wine or medium sherry

290ml/10fl oz/scant 1¼ cups double cream

1 Reserve 4 strawberries for decoration and put the rest in a blender. Purée until smooth, then press through a sieve into a clean bowl to remove the seeds. Stir in the icing sugar and set aside.

2 Put the caster sugar, Marsala wine and 1 teaspoon hot water in a large bowl and stir until the sugar dissolves. Add the cream and, using a balloon whisk, whip until it forms soft peaks.

3 Spoon a large spoonful of the strawberry purée into a small tall glass or bowl and top with some of the cream mixture. Layer again with the remaining purée and cream. I like to use uneven layers for a more relaxed look. Chill the syllabubs for 30 minutes until set. Decorate with the reserved strawberries and serve.

PINEAPPLE SORBET WITH LEMONGRASS AND MINT CRUSH

This refreshing sorbet is perfect after a spicy meal. Whisked egg white gives it a lighter texture, but you can leave it out, if you prefer.

SERVES 4

1 large pineapple, peeled, cored and cut into chunks, reserving any juice (about 500g/1lb 2oz prepared fruit)

55g/2oz root ginger, peeled and grated

40g/1½ oz stem ginger in syrup, (drained weight) finely chopped, with 1 tbsp of the syrup reserved

4 tbsp golden caster sugar

1 egg white

LEMONGRASS AND MINT CRUSH

1 handful of mint leaves, chopped

1 lemongrass stalk, outer layer removed and finely chopped

70g/2½ oz/scant ⅓ cup golden caster sugar

1 Put the pineapple and any juice in a food processor or blender and blend to a coarse purée, then transfer to a mixing bowl.

2 Using your hands, squeeze the grated ginger to extract the juice into the mixing bowl, discarding the pulp. Add the stem ginger, reserved ginger syrup and caster sugar and mix well. Pour the mixture into a sorbetière or 1l/35fl oz/4-cup freezer-proof container with a lid and freeze for 2 hours.

3 In a clean bowl, whisk the egg white until soft peaks form. Remove the mixture from the freezer and, if making by hand, stir with a fork to break up the ice crystals. Fold in the egg white, then return to the freezer and freeze for 3–4 hours until frozen.

4 Remove the sorbet from the freezer 20 minutes before serving. Using a mortar and pestle, crush the mint leaves, then add the lemongrass and continue crushing until the mixture forms a coarse paste. Add the sugar and grind until well mixed. Serve the pineapple sorbet in scoops with the lemongrass and mint crush sprinkled over the top.

Grilling lends foods a rich, toasted flavour and draws out the natural sugars in many fruits, vegetables and cheeses to yield a slightly sweet, often caramelized note. From delicately browned frittatas and tortillas to crisp golden burgers and desserts, the recipes in this chapter exemplify the true versatility of grilling.

GRILL

Warm Halloumi, Asparagus and Broad Bean Salad with Chipotle Dressing, page 58

BLACK BEAN, JALAPEÑO AND MOZZARELLA QUESADILLAS

SERVES 2

1 tbsp olive oil, plus extra for
   brushing
1 red onion, chopped
1 garlic clove, chopped
1 red pepper, deseeded and sliced
1 jalapeño chilli, deseeded and
   chopped
400g/14oz tinned black beans,
   drained
2 large soft tortillas
50g/1¾ oz mozzarella cheese,
   drained and sliced
salt and freshly ground black pepper

1 Heat the oil in a large non-stick frying pan over a medium-low heat
   and fry the onion for 8–10 minutes until softened. Add the garlic,
   red pepper and jalapeños and cook for another 2 minutes, stirring
   occasionally. Stir in the black beans and heat through, then roughly
   mash with a fork.

2 Preheat the grill to medium-high and line the grill pan with foil.
   Spoon the bean mixture on top of one of the tortillas and cover with
   the mozzarella and then with the second tortilla. Press the edges
   down slightly to encase the filling, then brush the top with oil.

3 Grill the quesadilla for 4–5 minutes until golden and crisp then
   carefully turn it over, using a spatula or palette knife, and cook for
   another 4 minutes. Cut into wedges and serve hot.

GOLDEN TOFU AND SMOKED PAPRIKA CORN SALAD

SERVES 4

2 corn on the cob, husks removed
1 tsp smoked paprika
2 large handfuls of rocket leaves
1 large handful of spinach leaves
leaves from 3 coriander sprigs
leaves from 3 mint sprigs
4 tomatoes, deseeded and diced
2 lavash flatbreads or tortillas

GOLDEN TOFU
1 tbsp balsamic vinegar
1 tbsp olive oil, plus extra for
   brushing
2 tbsp clear honey
2 tbsp tomato ketchup
1 tbsp light soy sauce
250g/9oz firm tofu, cut into 8 slices

DRESSING
3 tbsp extra-virgin olive oil
1 tbsp apple cider vinegar
1 small garlic clove, crushed
salt and freshly ground black pepper

1 To make the golden tofu, mix together the balsamic vinegar, olive
   oil, honey, ketchup and soy sauce in a dish. Add the tofu and turn to
   coat, then leave to marinate for at least 30 minutes.

2 Meanwhile, make the dressing. Whisk together the extra-virgin olive
   oil and cider vinegar in a small bowl. Add the garlic and season with
   salt and pepper, then set aside.

3 Preheat the grill to high and brush the grill rack with oil. Brush the
   corn with oil, then dust lightly with the paprika. Grill for 20 minutes,
   turning occasionally, until tender and blackened in places. Grill the
   tofu alongside the corn for 20 minutes, turning once and brushing
   with more of the marinade, until golden.

4 Meanwhile, toss the rocket, spinach, coriander and mint together
   in a serving bowl. Add the dressing and toss well. Slice the corn
   kernels away from the cobs and sprinkle them over the salad, along
   with the tomatoes. Divide on to four plates and top each portion
   with 2 slices of the tofu.

5 Lightly brush the flatbreads with oil and grill for 2 minutes until
   crisp, then sprinkle with salt and cut into wedges. Serve with
   the salad.

TEMPEH TIKKA KEBABS WITH MANGO DIPPING SAUCE

Don't be put off by the long list of ingredients in this recipe – most are store cupboard staples, and the tikka marinade can be whipped up in a few minutes. Tempeh is perfect for kebabs as it holds its shape during cooking and readily takes on stronger flavours, such as spices. If using wooden skewers, soak them in water for 30 minutes before using, to prevent them from burning.

SERVES 4

400g/14oz tempeh
150ml/5fl oz/scant ⅔ cup thick natural yogurt
4 tbsp mango chutney
1 heaped tsp peeled, grated root ginger

TIKKA PASTE

2 tsp ground coriander
2 tsp ground cumin
2 tsp turmeric
2 tsp ground ginger
1 tbsp paprika
½ tsp hot chilli powder
2 tbsp sunflower oil
3 garlic cloves, crushed
1 tbsp tamarind paste
3 tbsp thick natural yogurt
salt

RED ONION AND RADISH SALAD

1 red onion, thinly sliced into rounds
1 small cucumber, sliced into ribbons
8 radishes, sliced
lime juice, to taste
1 small handful of coriander leaves

1 Steam the tempeh for 10 minutes until softened slightly – this also removes any trace of bitterness. Remove from the steamer and cut into 32 cubes, each about 2cm/¾ in. Mix together all of the ingredients for the tikka paste and 2 tablespoons water in a large shallow dish. Add the tempeh and turn until coated in the paste, then set aside to marinate for at least 1 hour.

2 Preheat the grill to high and line the grill pan with foil. Thread 4 chunks of tempeh on to each of 8 skewers and grill for 8–10 minutes, turning occasionally, until slightly blackened in places.

3 Meanwhile, mix the yogurt, mango chutney and ginger together in a small bowl to make a dipping sauce and set aside.

4 To make the salad, arrange the onion, cucumber and radishes in a shallow bowl and squeeze some lime juice over the top. Season with salt and sprinkle with the coriander leaves. Serve the kebabs with the salad and dipping sauce.

SMOKED CHEDDAR TARTINES WITH PEAR CHUTNEY

SERVES 4

4 thick slices of crusty wholemeal
    bread
150g/5½oz/heaped 1¼ cups
    grated smoked Cheddar cheese
2 eggs, lightly beaten
2 tsp grainy mustard
salt and freshly ground black pepper
1 recipe quantity Pear Chutney
    (see page 180), to serve

1 Preheat the grill to medium-high. Grill one side of the bread
  until toasted.
2 Mix together the Cheddar, eggs and mustard and season with salt
  and pepper. Spread the cheese mixture over the untoasted side of
  each slice of bread and arrange on a grill pan. Grill for 7 minutes
  until bubbling and golden. Serve the tartines with a good spoonful
  of the pear chutney.

THAI TOFU CAKES WITH CHILLI DIPPING SAUCE

SERVES 4

500g/1lb 2oz firm tofu, patted dry
    and coarsely grated
3 large garlic cloves, finely chopped
2 red chillies, deseeded and finely
    chopped
2 lemongrass stalks, finely chopped
    with outer leaves removed
2 kaffir lime leaves, finely chopped
4cm/1½in piece of root ginger,
    peeled and coarsely grated
4 spring onions, finely chopped
4 tbsp chopped coriander leaves,
    plus extra to serve
1 large egg white
4 tbsp plain flour
salt and freshly ground black pepper
sunflower oil, for brushing

CHILLI DIPPING SAUCE
4 tbsp mirin
4 tbsp rice vinegar
2 spring onions, finely sliced
1 tbsp caster sugar
2 red chillies, deseeded and finely
    chopped
3 tbsp chopped coriander leaves

1 In a small bowl, mix together all of the ingredients for the chilli
  dipping sauce and set aside.
2 Squeeze the tofu in your hands to remove any excess water and put
  it in a mixing bowl. Add the garlic, chillies, lemongrass, lime leaves,
  ginger, spring onions, coriander leaves, egg white and flour. Season
  with salt and pepper and mix well. Shape the mixture into 16 tofu
  cakes of equal size, then cover and chill for 30 minutes to firm up.
3 Preheat the grill to high and line the grill pan with foil. Brush each
  tofu cake with sunflower oil and grill for 5–7 minutes on each side
  until golden, grilling in batches if necessary. Sprinkle with extra
  coriander leaves and serve warm with the chilli dipping sauce.

AUBERGINE, SCAMORZA AND BASIL ROLLS

SERVES 4

2 aubergines, trimmed and each one
cut lengthways into 6 slices
100ml/3½ fl oz/scant ½ cup olive
oil
3 tbsp pine nuts
200g/7oz scamorza (smoked
mozzarella cheese) cut into
8 slices
4 large tomatoes, each cut into
4 slices
8 large basil leaves
balsamic vinegar, for drizzling
salt and freshly ground black pepper

1 Preheat the grill to high and line the grill rack with foil. Discard the outermost slices of aubergine and liberally brush the remaining ones with oil. Grill for 12 minutes, turning once and brushing again with oil, if necessary, until tender and golden.

2 Meanwhile, toast the pine nuts in a dry frying pan over a medium-low heat, stirring occasionally, for 3–4 minutes until light golden. Watch carefully as they burn easily.

3 Put 1 slice of scamorza, 2 slices of tomato and 1 basil leaf in the centre of each slice of grilled aubergine and season with salt and pepper. Roll the aubergine over the filling and grill, seam-side down, for 5 minutes or until the mozzarella begins to melt and ooze out.

4 Serve with a drizzling of olive oil and balsamic vinegar and topped with the pine nuts.

ARTICHOKE, TOMATO AND BLACK OLIVE CROSTINI

Slicing the bread on the diagonal not only looks more attractive but you get a larger surface area for the topping. Rub the garlic over the toast while it's still warm – it literally melts into the surface of the bread, imparting a subtle flavour.

SERVES 4

1 small red onion, finely chopped
4 tomatoes, halved, deseeded and
diced
16 pitted black olives, finely
chopped
10 chargrilled artichoke halves,
halved
2 tbsp chopped flat-leaf parsley
leaves
2 tbsp chopped basil leaves
2 tbsp extra-virgin olive oil
8 thick slices of ciabatta or similar
open-textured bread
1 large garlic clove, halved
2 x 90g/3¼ oz rounds of goat's
cheese, sliced
salt and freshly ground black pepper

1 Preheat the grill to high. In a large bowl, mix together the onion, tomatoes, olives, artichokes, parsley and basil. Add the olive oil, season with salt and pepper and mix well.

2 Toast both sides of the bread under the grill until light golden and crisp. Rub one side of each slice of bread with the cut side of the garlic, then top with the goat's cheese. Grill for 3–4 minutes or until the cheese has melted, then remove from the grill.

3 Pile the tomato and artichoke mixture on top of the crostini and serve warm.

WARM HALLOUMI, ASPARAGUS AND BROAD BEAN SALAD WITH CHIPOTLE DRESSING

Halloumi is at its best when warm, so prepare it just before you serve this salad. Chipotles are smoked jalapeño chillies, and they lend a wonderful warmth to dishes. Here they are used in paste form, making a delicious smoky chilli marinade and dressing.

SERVES 4

4 tsp chipotle paste

5 tbsp extra-virgin olive oil

375g/13oz halloumi cheese, patted dry and sliced

20 asparagus, trimmed

900g/2lb broad beans, shelled

2 tbsp chopped parsley leaves

3 tbsp chopped coriander leaves

4 handfuls of rocket leaves

1 small red onion, thinly sliced into rounds

75g/2½oz sun-blush tomatoes in oil, drained and halved if large

1 small garlic clove, crushed

2 tbsp lemon juice

salt and freshly ground black pepper

1 Preheat the grill to high and line the grill pan with foil. Mix together the chipotle paste and 3 tablespoons of the olive oil in a shallow bowl. Add the halloumi and turn until coated, then set aside.

2 Brush the asparagus with 1 tablespoon of the remaining oil and grill for 5–7 minutes, turning once, until tender. Remove from the heat and set aside, but do not turn off the grill.

3 Meanwhile, boil the broad beans for 3–5 minutes until tender, then drain and refresh under cold running water. Pop the beans out of and discard their outer shells, then put the beans in a bowl with the parsley and coriander.

4 Divide the rocket leaves on to four plates and sprinkle the red onion and sun-blush tomatoes over them.

5 Remove the halloumi from the marinade and grill for 3 minutes on each side until softened. Mix the marinade with the remaining olive oil, garlic and lemon juice and season with salt and pepper. Pour it over the broad beans and toss well. Spoon the mixture over the rocket leaves, top with the halloumi and asparagus and serve.

GRILLED MUSHROOMS WITH CHICKPEA MASH
AND AUBERGINE SCHNITZEL

Grilling helps to seal in the mushroom juices, keeping them succulent and moist, while the combination of Parmesan cheese and matzo meal gives a crisp, crunchy coating to the slices of grilled aubergine.

SERVES 4

4 tbsp olive oil
2 tbsp balsamic vinegar
4 large portobello mushrooms, stalks discarded
1 aubergine, cut lengthways into 6 slices, discarding the outermost slices
50g/1¾oz/scant ½ cup finely grated Parmesan cheese
6 tbsp fine matzo meal
salt and freshly ground black pepper

SALSA VERDE

15g/½oz basil leaves, plus 4 extra leaves
1 large garlic clove, crushed
4 tbsp olive oil
1 tbsp lemon juice

CHICKPEA MASH

1 tbsp olive oil
2 garlic cloves, crushed
400g/14oz/2¼ cups cooked chickpeas
100ml/3½fl oz/scant ½ cup milk

1 First make the salsa verde. Put the basil, garlic, olive oil and lemon juice in a food processor and process until smooth. Season with salt and pepper and set aside.

2 Preheat the grill to high and line the grill pan with foil. Combine the olive oil and balsamic vinegar in a bowl and brush the mixture over the gills of the mushrooms. Grill, gill-side up, for 5 minutes, then turn over and brush the caps with a little more of the oil mixture and grill for another 5 minutes until softened. Wrap the mushrooms in foil and set aside to keep warm.

3 Meanwhile, make the chickpea mash. Heat the olive oil in a pan over a low heat and fry the garlic for 1 minute. Add the chickpeas and milk, heat through and then remove from the heat. Mash coarsely and season with salt and pepper. Cover with a lid and set aside to keep warm.

4 Brush one side of the aubergine slices with the oil and balsamic vinegar mixture. Mix the Parmesan and matzo meal together on a plate and season with salt and pepper, then press the oiled aubergines into the crumb mixture. Grill, crumb-side up, for 5 minutes until golden and crisp on the outside. Turn over, brush again with the oil mixture and sprinkle with the remaining Parmesan and matzo meal until covered. Grill for another 5 minutes.

5 To serve, put 1 mushroom, gill-side up, on each of four plates and top with the chickpea mash. Fold each aubergine slice in half and put it on top of the mash. Top each aubergine with a basil leaf, then drizzle the salsa verde around the mushrooms and serve immediately.

SPANISH EGG GRATIN

Smoked paprika is synonymous with Spanish cooking. Made from the ground dried pods of smoked red chillies, the spice lends a hot, rich smokiness to dishes.

SERVES 4

250g/9oz spinach leaves, tough
  stalks removed
2 tbsp olive oil
1 large onion, chopped
2 large garlic cloves, chopped
1 red pepper, deseeded and chopped
625ml/21 ½ fl oz/2 ½ cups passata
1 tbsp tomato paste
2 tsp dried oregano
1–2 tsp smoked paprika, to taste
8 eggs
70g/2 ½ oz/heaped ½ cup grated
  mature Cheddar cheese
salt and freshly ground black pepper
2 tbsp chopped parsley, to serve

GARLIC BRUSCHETTA

200g/7oz loaf of ciabatta, cut in
  half horizontally, then cut into
  quarters
olive oil, for brushing
2 garlic cloves, halved

1 Steam the spinach for 3–4 minutes until wilted and tender, then squeeze out any excess water and set aside.

2 Heat the olive oil in a large sauté pan over a medium-high heat and fry the onion for 8 minutes until softened. Add the garlic and red pepper and cook for another 2 minutes. Stir in the passata, tomato paste, oregano and 1 teaspoon of the paprika. Taste and add the remaining paprika if you want a spicier sauce. Bring to the boil, then reduce the heat to low and simmer for 10 minutes until reduced and thickened.

3 Preheat the grill to medium-high. Spread the cooked spinach in an even layer in a large, shallow flameproof dish. Spoon the tomato sauce over the spinach and make 8 indentations in the top. Break an egg into each indentation, then grill for 5 minutes until the eggs are almost cooked but the yolk remains runny.

4 Sprinkle the cheese over the top of the dish and grill for another 2 minutes until melted and golden.

5 While the gratin is cooking, heat a griddle pan over a medium-high heat. Brush both sides of the ciabatta with olive oil and griddle in two batches for about 8 minutes, turning halfway, or until crisp and golden. Rub the cut-side of the garlic over the toasted bread. Sprinkle the egg gratin with the parsley and serve with the garlic toast.

POLENTA BRUSCHETTA WITH ROSEMARY, TOMATO AND CANNELLINI BEANS

Polenta can be left to set, then cut into slices that are perfect for grilling. They take on a crisp texture and golden colour and are a great base for toppings.

SERVES 4

175g/6oz/1 heaped cup instant polenta

40g/1½ oz butter, diced

50g/1¾ oz/½ cup finely grated Parmesan cheese, plus extra to serve

1 tsp dried chilli flakes

olive oil, plus extra for greasing and brushing

salt and freshly ground black pepper

ROSEMARY BEANS

3 tbsp olive oil

4 large garlic cloves, chopped

2 tbsp chopped rosemary leaves

300g/10½ oz/2 cups cooked cannellini beans

125g/4½ oz sun-blush tomatoes, coarsely chopped

2 tbsp lemon juice

150g/5½ oz/scant 3 cups baby spinach leaves

1 First make the polenta. Put 850ml/29fl oz/3½ cups water in a saucepan, gradually stir in the polenta and bring to the boil. Reduce the heat to low and simmer, stirring, for 8–10 minutes until thickened. Remove from the heat and stir in the butter, Parmesan and chilli flakes, then season with salt and pepper.

2 Lightly grease a baking tray with olive oil and spread the polenta into an even layer about 2cm/¾ in thick. Smooth the top and leave to cool and set at room temperature.

3 Preheat the grill to high. Cut the polenta into 4 squares, then cut each square in half diagonally. Brush the triangles with oil, arrange them on the grill rack and grill for 6 minutes on each side until crisp on the outside and golden in places. Work in batches, if necessary, keeping the grilled polenta warm while you finish making the rest.

4 To make the beans, heat the olive oil in a sauté pan over a medium-low heat and fry the garlic and rosemary for 30 seconds. Add the beans and sun-blush tomatoes and stir until heated through. Reduce the heat to low, stir in the lemon juice and spinach and continue cooking until the leaves are just wilted.

5 Serve 2 wedges of polenta per person, topped with the beans and sprinkled with extra Parmesan.

SPICED KOFTA WITH APPLE AND MINT RAITA

Grilling gives these lightly spiced kofta a crisp, golden exterior, but they still remain moist inside. The heat of the accompanying ginger–tomato sauce is tempered by the cooling apple and mint raita.

SERVES 4

2 courgettes, coarsely grated

1 onion, coarsely grated

480g/1lb 1oz/scant 3 cups cooked chickpeas

2 tsp ground cumin

2 tsp ground coriander

1 red chilli, deseeded and chopped

olive oil, for brushing

salt and freshly ground black pepper

1 recipe quantity Sesame Seed Naan (see page 72), to serve

GINGER–TOMATO SAUCE

1 onion, chopped

2 large garlic cloves, halved

5cm/2in piece of root ginger, peeled and chopped

2 tbsp sunflower oil, plus extra for brushing

1 tsp fennel seeds

1 tsp dried chilli flakes

250ml/9fl oz/1 cup passata

100ml/3 $\frac{1}{2}$ fl oz/scant $\frac{1}{2}$ cup vegetable stock

2 tsp lemon juice

$\frac{1}{2}$ tsp salt

APPLE AND MINT RAITA

1 red dessert apple, cored and coarsely grated

3 heaped tbsp chopped mint leaves

2 tsp lemon juice

100ml/3 $\frac{1}{2}$ fl oz/scant $\frac{1}{2}$ cup natural yogurt

1 Squeeze the grated courgettes in your hands to remove any excess water. Put them in a food processor and add the onion, chickpeas, cumin, coriander and chilli. Season with salt and pepper and process to make a coarse, thick paste. Shape the courgette mixture into 12 balls of equal size and chill for 30 minutes to firm up.

2 Meanwhile, make the sauce. Clean the food processor, then process the onion, garlic and ginger until smooth. Heat the sunflower oil in a pan over a medium-low heat and fry the onion mixture, stirring occasionally, for 6 minutes. Add the fennel seeds and chilli flakes and cook for 1 minute, then add the passata and stock. Bring to the boil, reduce the heat to low and simmer for 10 minutes until thickened. Stir in the lemon juice and season with salt and pepper.

3 Preheat the grill to high and line the grill rack with foil. Meanwhile, mix together all of the ingredients for the raita and set aside.

4 Brush the kofta with olive oil and grill for 6–8 minutes on each side until golden. Warm the naan bread and put on four plates, serve with the koftas and ginger–tomato sauce. Serve with the raita.

LEEK, APPLE AND CHEESE SAUSAGES WITH WATERCRESS SAUCE

A version of the traditional Welsh Glamorgan sausage, these golden crumb-coated ones feature grated apple and are served with creamy watercress sauce.

SERVES 4

200g/7oz/4¼ cups fresh white breadcrumbs

150g/5½oz/scant 1½ cups grated mature Cheddar cheese

1 small leek, very finely chopped

1 dessert apple, cored and grated

1 tsp dried thyme

1 tsp Dijon mustard

2 tbsp milk

2 eggs

olive oil, for brushing

300g/10½oz Savoy cabbage, stems removed and finely shredded

25g/1oz butter

2 tsp caraway seeds

salt and freshly ground black pepper

WATERCRESS SAUCE

150g/5½oz watercress, thick stems removed

25g/1oz butter

25g/1oz/¼ cup plain flour

300ml/10½fl oz/scant 1¼ cups milk

1 In a large bowl, mix 150g/5½oz/3 cups of the breadcrumbs with the cheese, leek, apple and thyme. Stir in the mustard, milk and 1 of the eggs and season with salt and pepper. Shape into 12 sausages of equal size and chill for 30 minutes to firm up.

2 Preheat the grill to high and line the grill pan with foil. Beat the remaining egg in a bowl and dip each sausage in it, then roll in the breadcrumbs to coat. Lightly brush the sausages with olive oil and grill for 12 minutes, turning occasionally, until light golden and crisp on the outside.

3 Meanwhile, make the sauce. Blanch the watercress in boiling water for 2 minutes, then drain and refresh under cold running water. Finely chop the leaves and set aside. Melt the butter in a heavy-based saucepan over a low heat, stir in the flour and cook, stirring, for 1 minute. Gradually whisk in the milk, increase the heat slightly and cook until thick, smooth and creamy. Season with salt and pepper, then stir in the watercress and warm through.

4 Put the cabbage and 2 tablespoons water in a saucepan and cook, covered, over a low heat for 2–3 minutes, stirring occasionally, until just tender. Add the butter and caraway seeds, season with salt and pepper and stir until the cabbage is coated.

5 Divide the cabbage on to four plates and top each portion with 3 sausages. Serve with a spoonful of the watercress sauce on the side.

CASHEW AND CARROT BURGERS WITH PISTACHIO AND CHILLI CHUTNEY

Far removed from the archetypal vegetarian nut cutlet, these burgers have a light texture and slight Indian spiciness. The chutney adds just the right amount of piquancy and a delightful vibrant colour.

SERVES 4

150g/5½ oz/scant 1 cup cashew nuts
1 tbsp sunflower oil, plus extra for brushing
1 onion, finely chopped
2 tsp cumin seeds
2 tsp fenugreek seeds
1 tsp ground coriander
2 large garlic cloves, finely chopped
2 carrots, grated
50g/1¾ oz/scant 1 cup fresh breadcrumbs
1 egg, lightly beaten
1 heaped tbsp natural yogurt
flour, for dusting
salt and freshly ground black pepper
1 recipe quantity Sesame Seed Naan (see page 72), to serve

PISTACHIO & CHILLI CHUTNEY

4 tbsp shelled pistachios
1 green chilli, chopped
2 handfuls of coriander leaves
2 handfuls of mint leaves
1 tsp caster sugar
1 garlic clove, crushed
2 tbsp peeled and grated root ginger
juice of 1 lime

1 Preheat the oven to 180°C/350°F/gas 4. Put the cashew nuts on a baking tray and roast for 6–8 minutes until light golden all over. Leave to cool.

2 Heat the sunflower oil in a frying pan and fry the onion for 6 minutes, stirring occasionally, until softened. Add the cumin and fenugreek seeds and fry for another 1 minute, then stir in the ground coriander.

3 Grind the cashew nuts in a food processor until finely chopped, then transfer to a mixing bowl. Add the onion mixture, garlic, carrots, breadcrumbs, egg and yogurt. Season with salt and pepper and mix well. With floured hands, divide the mixture into 4 pieces, shape them into burgers and lightly coat in the flour. Chill for 30 minutes.

4 Meanwhile, make the pistachio and chilli chutney. Put the pistachios in a food processor and process until ground. Add the chilli, coriander and mint leaves, sugar, garlic, ginger, lime juice and 3 tablespoons water. Season with salt and pepper and process to a smooth purée the consistency of mayonnaise, adding more water if necessary.

5 Preheat the grill to high and line the grill rack with foil. Brush the tops of the burgers with oil and grill for 8–10 minutes, turning halfway and brushing with more oil, until golden.

6 Warm the naan breads and split them open. Put a burger on one half, top with a generous spoonful of the chutney. Cover with the other half of the naan and serve.

| GRILL

SPICED POTATO CAKES WITH HALLOUMI AND PINEAPPLE RELISH

It's best not to over-boil the potatoes for these golden potato cakes – you want to cook them until they are slightly *al dente* and then leave them to dry thoroughly in the pan before grating. This will help them to hold together when forming into cakes.

SERVES 4

1kg/2lb 4oz potatoes, peeled and
    quartered, if large
1 heaped tbsp cumin seeds
1 courgette, grated
1 tsp turmeric
25g/1oz butter, melted
plain flour, for dusting
400g/14oz halloumi cheese, drained
    and cut into 12 slices
large handful of rocket leaves
salt and freshly ground black pepper
alfalfa sprouts, to serve

PINEAPPLE RELISH

250g/9oz pineapple, diced
4 tbsp chopped coriander leaves
3 tbsp chopped mint leaves
1 long red chilli, deseeded and finely
    chopped
2 tbsp extra-virgin olive oil, plus
    extra for brushing

1 Cook the potatoes in boiling salted water for about 10 minutes until tender. Drain and leave to dry in the pan until cool enough to handle. Meanwhile, toast the cumin seeds in a dry frying pan over medium-low heat, stirring occasionally, for 2–3 minutes until light golden. Watch carefully as they burn easily.

2 Grate the potatoes into a bowl, add the cumin seeds, courgette, turmeric, salt and pepper to taste, and butter and stir until combined. Shape the mixture into 4 large cakes, put them on a lightly floured plate and chill for 30 minutes.

3 Meanwhile, to make the pineapple relish, mix together all of the ingredients in a bowl, season with salt and set aside.

4 Preheat the grill to high and line the grill rack with foil. Lightly brush the foil with olive oil and put the potato cakes on it, then lightly brush the top of the cakes with oil. Grill for 20 minutes until golden and crisp, turning the cakes over halfway through and brushing with a little more oil, if necessary.

5 While the potato cakes are cooking, heat a griddle pan over a medium-high heat until hot. Brush the halloumi with oil and griddle it for 2–3 minutes on each side.

6 Put 1 potato cake on each of four plates. Top with a handful of rocket leaves, 3 slices of halloumi and a spoonful of pineapple relish, then sprinkle with alfalfa sprouts and serve.

VEGETABLE AND MOZZARELLA TORTAS WITH AVOCADO CREAM

Layers of grilled vegetables interspersed with creamy mozzarella make this a pretty, summery dish. Don't worry if you don't have presentation rings — you can simply layer the tortas on the plate for a more relaxed look. While this is an easy recipe to prepare, it does require some patience as the vegetables need to be grilled in batches. They could also be roasted in the oven.

SERVES 4

125ml/4fl oz/½ cup olive oil, plus extra for brushing and drizzling
5 tbsp balsamic vinegar
3 courgettes, thinly sliced lengthways
1 large aubergine, thinly sliced lengthways, then each slice halved
1 large fennel bulb, thinly sliced lengthways
1 red pepper, deseeded and thinly sliced lengthways
1 yellow pepper, deseeded and thinly sliced lengthways
4 seeded soft tortillas
2 x 125g/4½ oz balls of mozzarella cheese, drained, patted dry and cut into 16 slices
1 handful of basil leaves
salt and freshly ground black pepper

AVOCADO CREAM

1 large avocado
1 tbsp olive oil
½ –1 tsp harissa paste
1 tbsp lemon juice
1 tbsp natural yogurt

1 Preheat the grill to high and line the grill rack with foil. Mix together the olive oil and balsamic vinegar, then brush the courgettes with the mixture. Arrange half of the courgettes on the grill rack and grill for 10 minutes, turning once, until golden in places and softened. Brush with more of the oil mixture, if necessary. Repeat with the remaining courgettes, then set aside, covered with foil.

2 Brush the aubergine with the oil mixture and grill in batches for 12 minutes, turning once and brushing with more of the oil mixture, if necessary. Repeat with the fennel and peppers, grilling them for 5 minutes on each side.

3 While the vegetables are grilling, make the avocado cream. Cut the avocado in half, remove the stone and scoop the flesh into a blender. Add the oil, harissa paste, lemon juice, yogurt and 1 tablespoon water and blend until smooth. Season with salt and pepper, add more harissa, if desired, and transfer to a bowl.

4 Heat a little of the olive oil in a large, non-stick frying pan over a low heat, then wipe with a crumpled piece of kitchen towel to remove any excess. Add 1 tortilla and cook for about 5 minutes, turning once, until golden and crisp. Remove from the pan and cut into wedges. Repeat with the remaining tortillas.

5 To assemble, put a 10cm/4in presentation ring on a serving plate and set aside 4 basil leaves. Layer the grilled vegetables and mozzarella inside, starting with a slice of aubergine, followed by pepper, basil, mozzarella, courgette, more basil, fennel, more mozzarella and more basil. Repeat with a second layer, then carefully remove the ring and top the torta with a basil leaf. Repeat to make 4 tortas. Drizzle the tortas with oil, sprinkle with black pepper and serve with the avocado cream and tortilla crisps.

SESAME SEED NAAN

MAKES 8

350g/12oz/2¾ cups plain flour, plus extra for kneading

2 tsp caster sugar

1 tsp salt

1 tsp baking powder

185ml/6fl oz/¾ cup milk

3 tbsp sunflower oil, plus extra for greasing

3 tbsp black sesame seeds

25g/1oz butter, melted

1 Sift together the flour, caster sugar, salt and baking powder into a large mixing bowl. Mix well and then make a well in the centre. Mix together the milk and sunflower oil and pour it into the well. Slowly incorporate the flour mixture from the edge of the bowl into the wet ingredients to make a soft dough. Turn out and knead for 10 minutes on a lightly floured surface, adding a little more flour if the dough is too sticky. Put the dough into a clean, oiled bowl, cover with a clean, damp tea towel and leave to rest in a warm place for 35 minutes.

2 Preheat the grill to high and put a large baking sheet on the upper shelf of the oven. Divide the dough into 8 equal balls and, on a lightly floured surface, thinly roll each one out into a large teardrop shape. Sprinkle with the sesame seeds, then press them into the dough with damp hands.

3 Grill 2 naans at a time for 2–3 minutes, turning once, until puffed up and golden. Watch carefully so they do not burn. Brush with the melted butter and serve warm.

WINTER ORANGE SALAD

SERVES 4

3 tbsp pumpkin seeds

3 mandarin oranges, peeled and sliced into rounds

1 tbsp extra-virgin olive oil

1 tbsp clear honey

100g/3½oz mixed salad leaves, such as watercress, red chard and lamb's lettuce

1 fennel bulb, thinly sliced

70g/2½oz red cabbage, thinly shredded

LEMON AND MUSTARD DRESSING

3 tbsp extra-virgin olive oil

1 tbsp lemon juice

1 tsp wholegrain mustard

salt and freshly ground black pepper

1 Preheat the grill to high and line the grill rack with foil. Toast the pumpkin seeds in a dry frying pan over medium-low heat, stirring occasionally, 2–3 minutes until light golden. Watch carefully as they burn easily.

2 Arrange the mandarins on the grill rack, brush with the olive oil and drizzle with the honey. Grill for 3–5 minutes until glossy and slightly blackened in places but still retaining their shape. Remove from the grill and set aside to cool.

3 Meanwhile, whisk together all of the ingredients for the dressing and season with salt and pepper.

4 Mix together the salad leaves, fennel and red cabbage in a serving bowl. Drizzle the dressing over the salad and toss well. Arrange the mandarins on top, sprinkle with the pumpkin seeds and serve.

MIXED SWEET PEPPERS WITH CAPER AND HERB DRESSING

SERVES 4

1 red pepper, deseeded and
quartered
1 yellow pepper, deseeded and
quartered
1 orange pepper, deseeded and
quartered
olive oil, for brushing
1 small handful of basil leaves,
to serve

CAPER AND HERB DRESSING
3 tbsp extra-virgin olive oil
1 garlic clove, crushed
1 tbsp oregano leaves
1 tbsp capers, drained and rinsed
salt and freshly ground black pepper

1 Preheat the grill to high and line the grill rack with foil. Brush the
peppers with olive oil and, working in batches, if necessary, put
them on the foil and grill for 10–12 minutes, turning once, until
softened and blackened in places.

2 Meanwhile, whisk together all of the ingredients for the dressing
and season with salt and pepper.

3 As the peppers come out of the grill, put them in a paper bag and
leave to stand for 10 minutes. This will make them easier to peel.
Remove and peel off the skins.

4 Put the peppers in a shallow serving dish. Drizzle with the dressing
and top with the basil leaves. Serve at room temperature.

GRILLED FENNEL WITH PANGRATTATO

Fennel's aniseed flavour can be very dominant when raw, but it takes on a softer,
milder taste after cooking. Grilled until tender, it goes particularly well with the
crisp golden crumbs.

SERVES 4

3 fennel bulbs, thinly sliced
crossways
olive oil, for brushing
salt and freshly ground black pepper

LEMON AND CHILLI PANGRATTATO
2 thick slices of slightly stale white
bread, crusts removed
1 tbsp olive oil
15g/½ oz butter
finely grated zest of 1 small lemon
1 small red chilli, deseeded and
finely chopped

1 Preheat the grill to high and line the grill rack with foil. Brush
the fennel with olive oil and grill for 8–10 minutes, turning once,
until tender.

2 Meanwhile, put the bread in a food processor and process into
coarse crumbs. Heat the olive oil and butter in a frying pan over
a low heat. Add the breadcrumbs and fry, stirring frequently, for
5 minutes until golden and crisp. Stir in the lemon zest and chilli,
season with salt and pepper and then remove from the heat.

3 Arrange the fennel in a serving dish, top with the lemon and chilli
pangrattato and serve.

LEMON MERINGUE TARTS

A twist on the classic lemon meringue pie, these individual tarts have a buttery, ginger biscuit base and are topped with a swirl of light meringue that is grilled briefly to give a touch of colour – simply delicious.

SERVES 4

190g/6¾ oz ginger nut biscuits
110g/3¾ oz butter, plus extra for greasing
125ml/4fl oz/½ cup lemon juice
2 tsp cornflour
125g/4½ oz/heaped ½ cup golden caster sugar
1 large egg yolk, lightly beaten
2 large egg whites

1 Lightly grease four 8cm/3¼ in loose-bottomed flan tins. To make the base, pulse the ginger nut biscuits in a food processor until they form very fine crumbs. Melt 80g/2¾ oz of the butter in a pan, add the biscuit crumbs and stir until combined. Divide the mixture into the tins and press to line the base and sides. Chill for 20 minutes to firm up.

2 Meanwhile, mix together the lemon juice and cornflour in a saucepan. Add 70g/2½ oz/scant ⅓ cup of the caster sugar, then bring to the boil over a medium-low heat, stirring continuously. Reduce the heat to low and simmer, stirring, for 2 minutes or until thickened. Stir in the remaining butter and remove from the heat when melted. Spoon the lemon curd mixture into the biscuit bases, then return to the fridge and chill while you make the meringue.

3 Preheat the grill to medium. Whisk the egg whites in a clean mixing bowl until they form stiff peaks, then gradually whisk in the remaining sugar to make a glossy, firm meringue. Transfer to a piping bag with a plain nozzle and pipe the meringue on top of the lemon curd. If you don't have a piping bag, the meringue can simply be spooned on top of each tart in a peak.

4 Put the tarts on a baking sheet and grill for 1 minute until the meringue is golden in places but remains marshmallowy and soft inside. Watch carefully as it can easily burn. Return to the fridge for 20 minutes to cool and firm up the bases again, then remove from the tins and serve.

GRILLED PLUMS ON BRIOCHE WITH LAVENDER YOGURT

This is the perfect pudding for when you are looking for something sweet and indulgent but don't have much time on your hands.

SERVES 4

10 plums, halved and stoned
25g/1oz butter, melted
3 tbsp soft dark brown sugar
½ tsp cinnamon
4 thick slices of brioche

LAVENDER YOGURT

125ml/4fl oz/½ cup Greek yogurt
3 tbsp clear honey
a few dried lavender flowers

1 Preheat the grill to high and line a baking sheet with foil. To make the lavender yogurt, put the yogurt in a bowl and drizzle with the honey. Sprinkle a few lavender flowers over the top and set aside.

2 Put the plums, cut-side up, on the baking sheet and brush with the butter. In a small bowl, mix together the brown sugar and cinnamon, then sprinkle the mixture over the plums. Grill for 5 minutes until softened and caramelized in places.

3 Meanwhile, lightly toast the brioche.

4 Arrange the plums on top of the brioche and serve with the lavender yogurt.

CARAMELIZED APPLE WITH CAMEMBERT ON WALNUT TOASTS

This simple, delicious dish is sure to appeal to those who can't decide between a dessert and a cheese course. It also makes a good light lunch served with a watercress salad.

SERVES 4

8 thick slices of walnut bread
40g/1½ oz butter
3 tbsp clear honey, plus extra for drizzling
4 red dessert apples, sliced crossways into thin rounds and seeds removed
185g/6½ oz Camembert cheese, sliced

1 Preheat the grill to high and line a grill pan with foil. Toast both sides of the walnut bread until lightly toasted and golden, then set aside.

2 Meanwhile, heat the butter and honey in a small saucepan until melted, stirring occasionally. Arrange the apple slices on the grill pan (you will probably need to cook them in two batches) and brush them with the honey-butter. Grill for 2 minutes on each side until softened and slightly golden.

3 Arrange the apple slices on the walnut toasts and top with the slices of Camembert. Grill for another couple of minutes or until the cheese is bubbling and golden in places. Serve 2 toasts per person, drizzled with extra honey, if desired.

RASPBERRY CRÈME BRÛLÉES

The grill has to be very hot before caramelizing the sugar topping on this French classic. Spraying a mist of water over the brûlées before grilling encourages the caramelization process. A blowtorch is also great for this.

SERVES 4

400ml/14fl oz/generous 1½ cups double cream
3 tbsp milk
1 vanilla pod, split lengthways and seeds scraped out
175g/6oz/heaped ¾ cup caster sugar
5 egg yolks
175g/6oz/1 cup raspberries

1 Preheat the oven to 150°C/300°F/gas 2. Put the cream, milk and vanilla pod and seeds in a heavy-based saucepan and bring to the boil over a medium to medium-low heat.

2 Put 125g/4½oz/heaped ½ cup of the caster sugar in a mixing bowl and set the remaining 4 tablespoons aside. Add the egg yolks to the mixing bowl and whisk until combined, then add the cream mixture and stir until the sugar dissolves. Remove and discard the vanilla pod.

3 Divide the raspberries into four large ramekins and strain the cream mixture evenly over them. Put them in a deep baking dish and add enough hot water to come halfway up the sides of the ramekins. Bake for 30–35 minutes until almost set – they should still be a little wobbly. Set aside to cool.

4 Just before serving, preheat the grill to high. Sprinkle each brûlée with 1 tablespoon of the reserved caster sugar and spray lightly with a tiny amount of water to help it caramelize. Grill for 4–5 minutes until the sugar forms a layer of golden caramel. Watch carefully as the sugar can easily burn. Leave to cool for 5 minutes to allow the caramel to crisp, then serve. Or leave to cool completely and serve chilled.

ALMOND AND AMARETTI PEACH CRUMBLES

SERVES 4

4 tbsp blanched whole almonds
8 amaretti biscuits
25g/1oz butter, melted
2 tbsp maple syrup
4 peaches, halved and pitted
extra-thick double cream, to serve

1 Preheat the grill to medium and line the grill pan with foil. Lightly toast the almonds in a dry frying pan over a medium-low heat for 2–3 minutes, stirring occasionally. Take care as they burn easily. Leave to cool, then chop roughly.

2 Roughly crush the amaretti, then mix them with the almonds, melted butter and maple syrup.

3 Arrange the peaches, cut-side up, on the foil-lined pan. Heap the amaretti mixture on top of each peach half and grill for 3 minutes or until golden and beginning to crisp (they will crisp up further as they cool). Serve warm with a generous spoonful of cream.

This imaginative collection of delicious dishes draws on the many different frying techniques to give foods colour, crunch and flavour. From sizzling Asian stir-fries and crisp, deep-fried morsels to griddled bruschetta and irresistibly sweet treats, these recipes encompass a world of cooking.

FRY

Cinnamon-Dusted Doughnuts with Chocolate Sauce, page 119

PAN-PIZZA WITH CARAMELIZED ONIONS AND DOLCELATTE

This yeast-free pizza is fantastically simple. The base is cooked on the hob, while the topping can either be raw, as in this Southern Italian-inspired version, or browned under the grill.

SERVES 2
2 tbsp olive oil
150g/5½ oz/scant 1½ cups
   dolcelatte cheese, cut into
   bite-sized pieces
2 tomatoes, deseeded and diced
1 handful of rocket leaves
extra-virgin olive oil, for drizzling

PIZZA BASE
225g/8oz/scant 2 cups self-raising
   flour, plus extra for kneading
½ tsp salt
1 tsp oregano leaves
4 tbsp olive oil
freshly ground black pepper

CARAMELIZED ONIONS
1 tbsp olive oil
1 red onion, thinly sliced into rings
½ tsp soft light brown sugar

1 To make the caramelized onions, heat the olive oil in a non-stick frying pan and fry the onion over a medium-low heat for 8 minutes, stirring frequently, until softened and starting to brown. Stir in the brown sugar and cook, stirring, for another 3 minutes until sticky and golden, then set aside. Reduce the heat to low if the onions become too dark.

2 Meanwhile, make the base. Sift the flour and salt into a mixing bowl and stir in the oregano. Make a well in the centre, add 2 tablespoons of the olive oil and 100ml/3½ fl oz/scant ½ cup water and mix, first with a palette knife, then with your hands to shape the dough into a ball. Lightly knead the dough on a lightly floured work surface and roll it out to fit a 25cm/10in non-stick frying pan.

3 Heat 1 tablespoon of olive oil in the pan over a medium heat and spread the oil over the base, using a crumpled piece of kitchen towel. Put the dough in the pan and cook for 5 minutes until light golden underneath.

4 Remove from the heat, cover the pan with a plate and carefully flip it over to release the pizza base on to the plate. Pour the remaining tablespoon of oil into the pan, slip the pizza base into the pan, uncooked-side down, and cook for another 5 minutes until light golden.

5 Top with the caramelized onions, dolcelatte and tomatoes and season with pepper. Add the rocket leaves, drizzle with a little extra-virgin olive oil and serve.

THAI-SPICED POLENTA WITH SWEET CHILLI PAK CHOI

A fusion of flavours, this polenta, made with Thai spices, has an Asian twist.
Its soft, creamy texture is perfect with the crisp stir-fried vegetables.

SERVES 4

1l/35fl oz/4 cups vegetable stock
210g/7 ½ oz/heaped 1⅓ cups
   instant polenta
1 heaped tsp Thai 7-spice powder
20g/¾ oz butter

SWEET CHILLI PAK CHOI
2 tbsp sweet chilli sauce
2 tbsp light soy sauce
2 tsp sesame oil
2 tbsp groundnut oil
1 large onion, sliced
200g/7oz long-stem broccoli,
   trimmed
2 pak choi, halved or quartered, if
   large, white part sliced and leaves
   left whole
100g/3 ½ oz mangetout
3 garlic cloves, thinly sliced
2.5cm/1in piece of root ginger,
   peeled and grated
1 red chilli, deseeded and sliced into
   thin rounds (optional)

1 Put the stock in a saucepan, gradually stir in the polenta and bring
   to the boil. Reduce the heat to low and simmer, stirring, for 6–8
   minutes until thickened. Add the 7-spice powder and butter and stir
   until melted, then cover with a lid and set aside.

2 Mix together the sweet chilli sauce, soy sauce and sesame oil and
   set aside.

3 Heat a wok over a high heat, add the groundnut oil and fry the
   onion for 2 minutes. Add the broccoli and white part of the pak choi
   and stir-fry for another 2 minutes, then add the mangetout, garlic,
   ginger, chilli, if using, and green leaves of the pak choi. Stir-fry for
   2 minutes, add the sweet chilli sauce mixture and toss well.

4 Divide the polenta on to four plates, top with the vegetables and
   serve immediately.

GIANT COUSCOUS WITH GOLDEN AUBERGINE AND HALLOUMI

Giant couscous, otherwise known as Israeli couscous or mougrabieh, is becoming increasingly available in food shops. The Lebanese grains are about the size of a small pea and retain their shape more successfully after cooking than the tiny-grained Moroccan variety.

SERVES 2–4
250g/9oz/scant 1⅓ cups wholemeal giant couscous
1 tsp vegetable bouillon powder
5 tbsp olive oil, plus extra for brushing
1 large aubergine, cut into bite-sized cubes
2 tbsp pomegranate molasses or date syrup
1 large onion, chopped
3 garlic cloves, chopped
2 courgettes, diced
1 large red pepper, deseeded and diced
1 red chilli, deseeded and thinly sliced
1 tsp cumin seeds
2 tsp ras-el-hanout
150g/5½ oz baby spinach leaves
2 tbsp lemon juice
250g/9oz halloumi cheese, patted dry and sliced
3 tbsp chopped coriander leaves
2 tbsp chopped parsley leaves
salt and freshly ground black pepper

1 Put the couscous in a saucepan, add enough water to just cover and bring to the boil. Stir in the bouillon powder, then reduce the heat to low and simmer, covered, for 8–10 minutes until the stock is absorbed and the grains are tender but not mushy. Remove from the heat and set aside, covered, for 10 minutes.

2 Meanwhile, heat 3 tablespoons of the olive oil in a large, non-stick frying pan over a medium-low heat and sauté the aubergine, stirring continuously, for 15 minutes or until softened and golden. Add the pomegranate molasses and stir until the aubergine is coated and glossy. Transfer to a bowl and cover to keep warm.

3 Clean the frying pan, then heat the remaining oil over a medium-low heat and fry the onion for 10 minutes until golden. Add the garlic, courgettes, red pepper and chilli and fry for another 3 minutes until tender. Stir in the cumin seeds and ras-el-hanout, then add the spinach and cook for 2 minutes until wilted. Fluff up the couscous with a fork, then add it and the lemon juice to the vegetables and mix well until heated through. Season with salt and pepper.

4 Heat a griddle pan until hot. Brush the halloumi with a little oil and griddle for 2–3 minutes on each side until softened.

5 Top the couscous with the aubergine and halloumi, sprinkle with the coriander and parsley and serve.

SOUFFLÉ OMELETTE WITH GOAT'S CHEESE AND ROSEMARY PESTO

For a perfect souffle omelette, the egg whites must first be whisked to soft, light, fluffy peaks. This version is filled with goat's cheese and a pumpkin seed and rosemary pesto.

SERVES 2

3 eggs, separated
15g/½ oz butter
50g/1¾ oz soft goat's cheese, sliced
salt and freshly ground black pepper

PUMPKIN SEED AND ROSEMARY PESTO

leaves from 2 long rosemary sprigs
1 large handful of basil leaves
1 garlic clove, crushed
5 tbsp olive oil
30g/1oz/¼ cup pumpkin seeds, lightly toasted
3 heaped tbsp grated Parmesan cheese

1 To make the pesto, put the rosemary, basil, garlic and olive oil in a blender or food processor and pulse until coarsely chopped. Add the pumpkin seeds and process again until finely chopped. Transfer to a bowl, stir in the Parmesan and season with salt and pepper. Taste and add a little more oil, if necessary.

2 In a bowl, beat the egg yolks with a fork and season with salt and pepper. Whisk the egg whites in a clean bowl until they form soft peaks, then fold them into the egg yolks.

3 Preheat the grill to medium-high. Melt the butter in a large, non-stick, flameproof frying pan over a medium-low heat, tilting the pan to evenly coat the base. Add the egg mixture to the pan and spread out with a spatula to cover the base of the pan. Cook for 3 minutes until set and golden. Arrange the goat's cheese over the omelette and grill for 1–2 minutes, until the cheese melts.

4 Remove from the grill and spoon a few small dollops of the pesto down the centre. (The leftover pesto will keep for about 1 week in the fridge.) Carefully fold the omelette in half to enclose the filling, then cut in half crossways and serve.

JAPANESE ASPARAGUS EGG ROLLS

A Japanese omelette pan is rectangular, but you can also use a round pan to make these delicate, sushi-style vegetable rolls.

SERVES 4

1 tbsp sesame oil
1 tbsp mirin
12 asparagus spears, trimmed
2 tbsp groundnut oil
2 large shallots, finely chopped
5 spring onions, shredded
2 red chillies, deseeded and finely
  chopped
6 large eggs, lightly beaten
a few sprigs of coriander, coarsely
  chopped
salt and freshly ground black pepper
tamari soy sauce, to serve
pickled ginger, to serve

PICKLED VEGETABLE SALAD

13cm/5in piece of cucumber
1 carrot
3 tbsp rice wine vinegar
1 tbsp toasted nori flakes
1 tbsp sesame seeds, toasted

1 To make the pickled vegetable salad, cut the cucumber and carrot into ribbons, using a mandolin or vegetable peeler. Put them in a bowl, mix in the rice wine vinegar and season with salt. Divide the salad into four small serving bowls and sprinkle with the nori flakes and sesame seeds.

2 In a shallow dish, mix together the sesame oil and mirin, then add the asparagus and turn until coated. Heat a wok over a high heat and stir-fry the asparagus for 3 minutes or until tender. Remove from the wok and set aside.

3 Pour half of the groundnut oil into the wok and add the shallots, three-quarters of the spring onions and half of the chillies. Stir-fry for 1 minute, then remove from the wok and set aside.

4 Season the eggs with salt and pepper. Heat a Japanese omelette pan or a medium, non-stick frying pan with a little of the remaining oil over a medium-low heat. Add a quarter of the beaten egg and swirl it around to evenly cover the base of the pan. Cook for 1–2 minutes until set, then slide it out on to a plate. Cover to keep warm and set aside while you make 3 more omelettes, adding more oil to the pan as necessary.

5 Trim each omelette into a square, if necessary, and spoon a quarter of the shallot mixture down the centre of each one. Arrange 3 asparagus spears on top, then roll up the omelettes and cut each roll into 2.5cm/1in pieces.

6 Divide the omelette rolls on to four plates, standing them up on their ends. Sprinkle with the reserved spring onions, chilli and coriander and serve warm or at room temperature with tamari for dipping and pickled ginger and vegetables as accompaniments.

BLINIS WITH AUBERGINE CAVIAR AND HONEY FIGS

Just a smidgeon of oil is needed to fry these large blinis – you want the outside golden and crisp and the inside to remain light and fluffy. You can, of course, also make bite sized blinis and serve them topped in the same way as canapés.

SERVES 4

3 tbsp pine nuts
3 figs, sliced lengthways
clear honey, for brushing
sunflower oil, for frying
1 recipe quantity Aubergine Caviar
   (see page 222)
watercress, to serve

BLINI

100g/3½ oz/heaped ¾ cup plain
   flour
40g/1½ oz/⅓ cup buckwheat flour
½ tsp salt, plus extra to season
1 tsp dried active yeast
125ml/4fl oz/½ cup milk
5 tbsp soured cream
1 egg, separated

1 To make the blini batter, sift both flours into a mixing bowl and stir in the salt and yeast. Mix together the milk and soured cream in a small saucepan and heat gently until lukewarm – make sure it is not too hot or the yeast will die. Remove the pan from the heat, whisk in the egg yolk, then gradually stir the milk mixture into the dry ingredients to make a smooth, thick batter. Cover with a clean tea towel and leave to rest in a warm place for 30–45 minutes or until bubbles appear on the surface.

2 Meanwhile, toast the pine nuts in a non-stick frying pan over a medium-low heat for 2–3 minutes, stirring occasionally, until light golden, then set aside. Watch carefully as they burn easily.

3 Lightly oil the frying pan and cook the figs over a medium-low heat for 1 minute on each side, then reduce the heat to low, brush the figs with honey and cook for another 1–2 minutes on each side until golden and crisp.

4 When the batter is ready, whisk the egg white in a clean bowl until it forms soft peaks and fold it into the mixture. Heat a lightly oiled, large non-stick frying pan over a medium heat. For each blini, add 125ml/4fl oz/½ cup of the batter to the pan and cook for 2 minutes on each side until golden, reducing the heat if the blinis brown too quickly. (You may have some leftover batter.) Alternatively, make smaller blinis and cook them for 1 minute on each side.

5 Top each blini with a large spoonful of the aubergine caviar, followed by a few slices of fig. Sprinkle with the pine nuts and serve with watercress.

SPICED PEAR AND PECAN SALAD WITH POLENTA CROÛTONS

For the best results, use slightly under-ripe pears so they retain their shape when frying them in the spiced honey glaze. This substantial salad is a fabulous combination of colour, flavour and texture.

SERVES 4

25g/1oz butter
2 slightly under-ripe pears, peeled, each cut into 8 wedges and cored
1 tsp ground ginger
2 tsp clear honey
150g/5½oz rocket leaves
100g/3½oz watercress
50g/1¾oz/½ cup pecans, toasted
85g/3oz dolcelatte cheese, cut into bite-sized pieces

DRESSING

4 tbsp extra-virgin olive oil
1 tbsp lemon juice
2 tsp Dijon mustard
salt and freshly ground black pepper

POLENTA CROÛTONS

60g/2¼oz/scant ½ cup instant polenta
20g/¾oz butter
1 large pinch dried chilli flakes
2 tbsp olive oil, plus extra for greasing

1 First make the polenta croûtons. Put 290ml/10fl oz/scant 1¼ cups water in a saucepan and sprinkle in the polenta, bring to the boil, stirring frequently. Reduce the heat to low and simmer for 6–8 minutes until thickened. Remove from the heat, stir in the butter and chilli and season with salt and pepper. Lightly grease a medium baking tin and spread out the polenta to about 1cm/½in thick. Smooth the top and chill until set, then cut the polenta into 1cm/½in cubes.

2 Heat half of the olive oil over a medium-high heat in a large, non-stick frying pan. Fry half of the polenta croûtons for 12–15 minutes, turning regularly, until crisp all over, then drain on kitchen paper. Repeat with the remaining oil and croûtons, then set aside.

3 Wipe the pan with kitchen paper and melt the butter over a medium-low heat, then fry the pears for 3–5 minutes, turning once. Add the ginger and honey, turn the pears to coat in the mixture and cook for another 1 minute until golden.

4 Mix together all of the ingredients for the dressing and season to taste with salt and pepper. Divide the rocket and watercress on to four plates and drizzle with the dressing. Sprinkle the pecans over the leaves and top with the pears, dolcelatte and polenta croûtons, then serve.

AKOORI WITH POTATO AND MUSTARD SEED PARATHA

Traditional Indian scrambled egg, akoori is flavoured with chilli, ginger and coriander. As with any version of scrambled egg, the secret is not to overcook it as the egg becomes tough and rubbery.

SERVES 4

55g/2oz butter
1 tsp cumin seeds
4 spring onions, thinly sliced
1 green chilli, deseeded and chopped
1 red pepper, deseeded and diced
2.5cm/1in piece of root ginger, peeled and finely chopped
8 eggs, lightly beaten
3 tomatoes, peeled, deseeded and diced
2 tbsp chopped coriander leaves
freshly ground black pepper

POTATO AND MUSTARD SEED PARATHA

200g/7oz/heaped 1½ cups plain flour, plus extra for kneading
½ tsp salt, plus extra to season
2 tbsp sunflower oil, plus extra for greasing
125g/4½oz potatoes, peeled and quartered, if large
1 small onion, finely chopped
2 tsp black mustard seeds
½ tsp ground turmeric

1 To make the paratha, sift the flour and salt into a mixing bowl, stir well and then make a well in the centre. Pour 125ml/4fl oz/ ½ cup lukewarm water and half of the sunflower oil into the well and stir with a fork until combined, then use your hands to shape the mixture into a ball of soft dough. It should be fairly sticky. Add a little extra water if the dough is too dry.

2 Turn out the dough and knead on a lightly floured work surface for 5 minutes until smooth, then transfer to a lightly greased mixing bowl, cover with a clean damp tea towel and leave to rest for 30 minutes. Meanwhile, boil the potatoes until tender, drain and mash, then leave to cool.

3 Heat a frying pan over a medium heat. Add the remaining sunflower oil, reduce the heat to medium-low and fry the onion for 6 minutes, stirring occasionally, until softened. Add the mustard seeds and cook for another 2 minutes, then stir in the turmeric. Add to the mashed potato and mix well to form a thick paste.

4 Divide the dough into 4 pieces and on a lightly floured surface roll 1 piece out into a 1cm/½in-thick circle. Spread 2 teaspoons of the potato mixture over one half, fold into a semicircle and then into quarters. Roll out again to about 20cm/8in in diameter and stretch into a teardrop shape. Pat off any excess flour and set the paratha aside while you repeat with the remaining dough and filling.

5 Heat a large, non-stick frying pan over a medium-low heat. Brush one side of a paratha with oil and cook, oiled-side down, for 2 minutes. Brush the top with a little more oil, turn over and cook for another 2 minutes until light golden. Wrap in foil and keep warm while you cook the remaining parathas.

6 To make the akoori, melt the butter in a non-stick frying pan over a medium-low heat. Add the cumin seeds, spring onions, chilli, red pepper and ginger and stir-fry for 1 minute. Season the eggs with salt and pepper and pour them into the pan. Using a spatula, gently stir for 3 minutes until the eggs are scrambled but still creamy, then gently stir in the tomatoes. Spoon the akoori over the paratha, sprinkle with the coriander and serve immediately.

THAI FRIED RICE WITH CRISP GINGER

Jasmine rice, with its soft, yielding texture and unassuming flavour, readily takes on the fragrant notes of lemongrass, ginger and chilli. For the best results, make sure the cooked rice is completely cool before stir-frying and the grains are as separated as possible.

SERVES 4

350g/12oz/1¾ cups Jasmine rice, rinsed
100ml/3½ fl oz/scant ½ cup sunflower oil
60g/2¼ oz root ginger, peeled and grated
4 tbsp toasted unsalted peanuts, brown skins rubbed off
2 tsp kecap manis
1 tbsp vegetarian fish sauce
2 tbsp light soy sauce
2 tsp lime juice
½ tsp caster sugar
6 spring onions, sliced diagonally
4 garlic cloves, chopped
1 long red chilli, deseeded and sliced
2 lemongrass sticks, outer leaves discarded, and finely chopped
leaves from a few coriander sprigs

1 Put the rice in a saucepan and cover with cold water by about 1cm/½ in. Bring to the boil, then reduce the heat to low. Simmer, covered, for 10 minutes until the rice is tender and the water is absorbed. Remove from the heat and leave to stand, covered, for 5 minutes. Spread the rice out on a baking tray and leave to cool completely.

2 In a wok, heat the sunflower oil to 180°C/350°F. Add half of the ginger and deep-fry for 2 minutes or until crisp and golden. Scoop out, using a slotted spoon, and drain on kitchen paper.

3 In a bowl, mix together the peanuts and kecap manis. Spoon 1 tablespoon of the oil from the wok into a frying pan, add the peanuts and fry over a medium-low heat for 2 minutes, turning once, until dark golden and sticky. Watch carefully as the nuts burn easily. If they are becoming too dark, reduce the heat to low. Remove from the heat and set aside. Mix together the vegetarian fish sauce, soy sauce, lime juice and caster sugar in a bowl and set aside.

4 Pour off all but 3 tablespoons of the oil from the wok. Add the remaining ginger, the white part of the spring onions, garlic, chilli and lemongrass and stir-fry over a high heat for 1 minute. Stir in the cold rice, breaking up any lumps. Add the fish sauce mixture and stir-fry until hot. Divide the rice into four bowls and sprinkle with the green part of the spring onions, peanuts and coriander leaves. Top with a pile of crispy ginger and serve.

STOVE-TOP SQUASH SCONES WITH CAVOLO NERO IN CIDER SAUCE

SERVES 4

250g/9oz butternut squash, peeled, deseeded and cut into bite-sized pieces

185g/6½oz/1½ cups plain flour

½ tsp salt

½ tsp bicarbonate of soda

1 tsp baking powder

80g/2¾oz butter

1 large egg, lightly beaten

2 tbsp milk

3 tbsp olive oil

2 leeks, sliced

350g/12oz cavolo nero, sliced crossways into thin strips

1 tbsp thyme leaves

200g/7oz/scant 1½ cups cooked butter beans

200ml/7fl oz/scant 1 cup dry cider

1 tsp Dijon mustard

4 tbsp double cream

salt and freshly ground black pepper

leaves from a few parsley sprigs, chopped

1 Steam the squash until tender, then transfer to a bowl, mash with a fork and set aside to cool.

2 Preheat the oven to 70°C/150°F/gas ¼. Sift the flour, salt, bicarbonate of soda and baking powder into a mixing bowl. Melt 50g/1¾oz of the butter and stir it into the dry ingredients, along with the mashed squash, egg and milk. Stir to make a soft dough.

3 Heat 1 tablespoon of the oil in a large, non-stick frying pan over a medium heat. Spoon a quarter of the dough into the pan and, using a spatula, flatten into a 1cm/½in-thick round. Repeat to add another scone to the pan, reduce the heat to medium-low and cook for 4–5 minutes on each side until golden. Reduce the heat to low if the scones are browning too quickly. Transfer to an ovenproof plate, cover with foil and keep warm in the oven while you cook the remaining 2 scones, adding another spoonful of oil to the pan. Keep the scones warm while you make the sauce.

4 Heat the remaining oil and butter in a large frying pan over a medium-low heat, fry the leeks for 4 minutes, stirring occasionally. Add the cavolo nero and thyme and cook, stirring, for 3 minutes, then stir in the butter beans and cider. Cook over a medium-high heat for 5–10 minutes until the cider has reduced by half. Reduce the heat to medium-low and stir in the mustard and cream. Season with salt and pepper and warm through. Serve the scones with the sauce and sprinkled with the parsley.

BARLEY WITH GARLIC, WATERCRESS AND MELTING CAMEMBERT

SERVES 4

275g/9¾oz/1¼ cups pearl barley

2 tbsp olive oil

2 large garlic cloves, coarsely chopped

2 tsp dried oregano

1 long red chilli, chopped

150g/5½oz watercress

1–2 tbsp lemon juice, to taste

200g/7oz Camembert cheese, rind discarded and cheese cut into bite-sized chunks

salt and freshly ground black pepper

1 Put the barley in a saucepan, cover with at least 750ml/26fl oz/3 cups water and bring to the boil. Reduce the heat to low and simmer, covered, for 25 minutes, or until the grains are tender, then drain and set aside.

2 Heat the oil in a large, non-stick frying pan over a low to medium heat and fry the garlic, oregano and chilli for 1 minute. Add the barley and stir until it is coated in the oil. Stir in the watercress and lemon juice and cook for 2–3 minutes until wilted. Add the Camembert and cook, stirring, until melted and the mixture is warmed through. Season with salt and pepper and serve.

YAKISOBA WITH TOFU AND GOLDEN CASHEWS

Yakisoba simply means stir-fried noodles, and this classic dish is bursting with fresh Asian flavours. A proper stir-fry should be piping hot, with the vegetables cooked through but still crunchy. Have all the ingredients measured and prepared before you start to cook, that way it takes only minutes from wok to plate.

SERVES 4

2 tbsp tamari soy sauce

1 tbsp sesame oil

6 tbsp teriyaki sauce

350g/12oz tofu, patted dry and cut into 1.5cm/⅝in cubes

4 tbsp cashew nuts

1 tbsp kecap manis

325g/11½ oz soba noodles

250g/9oz long-stemmed broccoli, ends trimmed

3 tbsp sunflower oil

1 large yellow pepper, deseeded and cut into strips

2 garlic cloves, finely chopped

2.5cm/1in root ginger, peeled and finely sliced

8 spring onions, sliced diagonally

freshly ground black pepper

2 tbsp pink pickled ginger, to serve

1 In a shallow bowl, mix together the tamari, sesame oil and teriyaki sauce. Add the tofu and turn to coat, then leave to marinate for at least 1 hour.

2 Toast the cashew nuts in a dry frying pan over a medium-low heat for 2–3 minutes, stirring occasionally, until golden. Transfer to a bowl, add the kecap manis and stir to coat the nuts. Return the nuts to the frying pan and cook for 1 minute, turning once, until golden and glossy. Watch carefully as they can easily burn. Remove the nuts from the pan, spread them out on a baking sheet and leave to cool.

3 Cook the soba noodles according to the packet instructions, adding the broccoli 2 minutes before the end of the cooking time. Drain and refresh under cold running water.

4 Heat a large wok over a high heat. Add 2 tablespoons of the sunflower oil and fry the tofu over a medium heat, reserving the marinade, for 8–10 minutes, turning occasionally, until golden. Remove from the wok and set aside, covered.

5 Wipe the wok with kitchen paper, then heat the remaining sunflower oil over a medium heat. Add the yellow pepper, garlic, ginger and the white part of the spring onions and stir well. Turn the heat down to medium-low and add the broccoli, noodles and reserved marinade. Stir until combined and warmed through, then season with pepper. Divide into four large, shallow bowls. Top with the tofu, nuts, the green part of the spring onions and the pickled ginger, then serve.

CARROT AND POTATO RÖSTI WITH EGG AND CARAMELIZED TOMATOES

SERVES 4

650g/1lb 7oz potatoes, peeled
2 carrots, peeled and grated
5 tbsp olive oil, for frying, plus extra
    if needed
4 eggs
salt and freshly ground black pepper

CARAMELIZED TOMATOES

5 tbsp olive oil
350g/12oz cherry tomatoes, halved
leaves from 4 thyme sprigs
2 tbsp balsamic vinegar

1 Boil the potatoes in salted water for about 8–10 minutes, then drain and leave to cool. Once cool, grate into a mixing bowl and add the carrots. Season with salt and pepper, mix well and shape into 8 rösti, each about 7cm/2¾in diameter and 2.5cm/1in thick.

2 Preheat the oven to 70°C/150°F/gas ¼. In a large, non-stick frying pan, heat 3 tablespoons of the olive oil over a medium heat. Working in batches, fry the rösti for 6 minutes on each side until crisp, reducing the heat to medium-low if they start to cook too quickly. Drain on kitchen paper, cover with foil and keep warm in the oven while you make the remaining rösti, adding more oil to the pan, if needed.

3 To make the caramelized tomatoes, heat the olive oil in a frying pan over a medium-low heat. Add the tomatoes and half of the thyme, cook for 1 minute, turning the tomatoes once, then add the balsamic vinegar. Reduce the heat to low and cook for 2 minutes, turning occasionally, until the tomatoes start to caramelize. Season to taste with salt and pepper and set aside.

4 To fry the eggs, add the remaining 2 tablespoons of the oil to the cleaned frying pan, if necessary. Crack the eggs into the pan and fry over a medium-low heat for 4 minutes, until the whites are cooked but the yolks are still runny. Serve 2 rösti per person, topped with 1 fried egg, sprinkled with the remaining thyme, and served with the tomatoes.

ORANGE AND TAMARI-GLAZED TEMPEH

SERVES 4

juice of 3 oranges
3 tbsp clear honey
3 tbsp tamari soy sauce
¼ tsp dried chilli flakes (optional)
cornflour, for dusting
400g/14oz tempeh, patted dry and
    cut into 5mm/¼in slices
125ml/4fl oz/½ cup sunflower oil
cooked rice, to serve

1 Mix together the orange juice, honey, tamari and chilli flakes, if using, then set aside.

2 Cover a small plate with cornflour. Dip both sides of each slice of tempeh into the cornflour to lightly coat.

3 Heat the sunflower oil in a large frying pan over a medium heat. Add half of the tempeh and fry for 8–10 minutes, turning once, until crisp and light golden. Remove the tempeh from the pan and drain on kitchen paper. Repeat with the remaining tempeh.

4 Drain the oil from the pan and return half of the tempeh. Add half of the orange juice mixture and cook over a medium-low heat for 2 minutes, turning once, until the liquid has thickened and the tempeh is glossy and golden. Keep warm while you cook the remaining tempeh. Serve hot with rice.

BLACK BEAN VEGETABLES WITH CRISP NOODLE NESTS

SERVES 4

3 tbsp Chinese black beans

2 tbsp soy sauce

1 tsp cornflour

375ml/13fl oz/1½ cups sunflower oil, for deep-frying

100g/3½ oz dry vermicelli rice noodles

280g/10oz long-stemmed broccoli, stems sliced and florets left whole

1 large yellow pepper, deseeded and sliced

6 spring onions, sliced diagonally

4 pak choi, stems sliced and leaves left whole

2 courgettes, sliced diagonally

2.5cm/1in piece of root ginger, peeled and cut into thin strips

2 large garlic cloves, finely chopped

2 tbsp Chinese cooking wine or dry sherry

1 tsp sesame oil

1 Put the black beans in a bowl, cover with boiled water and leave to soak for 30 minutes. Drain, reserving 3 tablespoons of the soaking liquid. Mix together the soy sauce, cornflour and reserved soaking water and set aside.

2 In a large wok, heat the sunflower oil to 180°C/350°F or until a cube of bread turns golden in 40 seconds. Add half of the noodles – they should puff up, becoming light and crisp as soon as they are immersed in the oil. Using a slotted spoon, remove the noodles from the wok and drain on kitchen paper. Set aside while you cook the remaining noodles.

3 Pour off all but 1 tablespoon of the oil from the wok and add the broccoli. Stir-fry over a high heat for 1 minute, then add the yellow pepper, spring onions, pak choi, courgette, ginger, garlic and black beans and stir-fry for another 2 minutes.

4 Reduce the heat to medium-low, add the Chinese wine, sesame oil and soy sauce mixture and stir-fry briefly until thickened slightly. Divide the stir-fry into four shallow bowls, top with the crisp noodles and serve immediately.

SPICED SWEET POTATO, COURGETTE AND RED PEPPER EGGAH

SERVES 4

355g/12½ oz sweet potatoes, peeled and halved or quartered

2 tbsp olive oil

15g/½ oz butter

1 onion, thinly sliced

1 courgette, diced

2 garlic cloves, finely chopped

1 small red pepper, deseeded and diced

a pinch of cayenne pepper

1 tsp cumin seeds

1 tsp coriander seeds, crushed

1 tsp dried thyme

6 eggs, lightly beaten

2 tbsp chopped coriander leaves

salt and freshly ground black pepper

1 Boil the sweet potatoes for 10 minutes until tender. Drain and leave to cool slightly, then cut into bite-sized cubes.

2 Preheat the grill to high. Heat the oil and butter in a large, ovenproof, non-stick frying pan over a medium heat. Fry the onion for 8 minutes, reducing the heat to medium-low, until softened. Add the courgette, garlic and red pepper and fry, stirring frequently, for another 4 minutes. Stir in the cayenne pepper, cumin and coriander seeds and thyme and cook for 1 minute. Stir in the sweet potatoes and spread the mixture out in an even layer in the pan.

3 Season the beaten eggs with salt and pepper, add the coriander leaves and pour the mixture over the vegetables. Cook over a medium-low heat for 3 minutes until the base is set and golden.

4 To cook the top, put the pan under the grill for 2 minutes until set and light golden. Cut into wedges and serve.

BRUSCHETTA WITH FETA, PUY LENTILS AND COURGETTE RIBBONS

This is not a dainty bruschetta, normally served as a nibble with drinks, but one of substance that makes a filling meal served with a crisp green salad. It's best to use an open-textured bread, for the bruschetta and griddling the slices lends a characteristic smoky flavour.

SERVES 4

175g/6oz/scant ¾ cup Puy lentils
8 thick slices of ciabatta or pain de campagne
olive oil, for brushing
2 courgettes, thinly sliced lengthways into ribbons
16 baby plum tomatoes, halved or quartered, if large
2 tbsp chopped parsley leaves
165g/5¾ oz feta cheese, diced

DRESSING

1 red chilli, deseeded and finely chopped
1 tbsp kecap manis
1 tbsp balsamic vinegar
2 tbsp extra-virgin olive oil, plus extra for drizzling (optional)
1–2 tbsp lemon juice
1 garlic clove, crushed
salt and freshly ground black pepper

1 Put the lentils in a saucepan and cover with water. Bring to the boil, then reduce the heat to low, cover partially and simmer for 25 minutes or until tender. Drain and transfer to a mixing bowl.

2 Meanwhile, heat a griddle pan over a medium heat until hot and brush the slices of bread with olive oil. Griddle 3 or 4 slices at a time, depending on their size and arranging them diagonally in the pan, for about 5–7 minutes, turning once until toasted. Keep warm while you griddle the remaining slices, then set aside.

3 To griddle the courgettes, brush them with a little oil, then arrange in the hot pan. Griddle for 8 minutes, turning once, until tender and charred in places.

4 When the lentils are cooked, mix together all of the ingredients for the dressing and pour it over the warm lentils. Add the tomatoes and parsley and toss well, then set aside.

5 Spoon the lentil mixture on top of the toasts and top with the feta and courgettes. Serve drizzled with extra olive oil, if desired.

VIETNAMESE COCONUT PANCAKES WITH VEGETABLE STIR-FRY

Coconut milk adds richness to these golden-coloured savoury pancakes. They are slightly thicker than traditional French crêpes and make a great base for the stir-fried vegetables in a sesame and ginger dressing featured here.

SERVES 4

1 tbsp sunflower oil, plus extra for frying

85g/3oz/½ cup cashew nuts

1 onion, sliced

175g/6oz mangetout, trimmed

1 large carrot, thinly sliced diagonally

150g/5½oz Chinese leaves, shredded

1 garlic clove, crushed

1 tbsp peeled and grated root ginger

sesame oil, for drizzling

2 tbsp chopped coriander leaves

2 tbsp torn basil leaves

2 tbsp chopped mint leaves

COCONUT PANCAKES

200g/7oz/scant 1¼ cups rice flour

½ tsp salt

1 tsp ground turmeric

1 egg, lightly beaten

400g/14oz/scant 1⅔ cups coconut milk

SESAME AND GINGER DRESSING

1 tbsp rice wine vinegar

juice of 1 lime

2 tbsp kecap manis

1 tbsp sesame oil, plus extra for drizzling

1 tbsp soft brown sugar

1 tbsp peeled and grated root ginger

1 small red chilli, finely chopped

1 garlic clove, crushed

½ tsp salt

1 To make the pancakes, sift the rice flour, salt and turmeric into a bowl. Slowly whisk in the egg, coconut milk and 4 tablespoons water to make a smooth, thin batter the consistency of single cream. Leave to stand for 30 minutes.

2 Meanwhile, mix together all of the ingredients for the dressing in a small bowl and set aside.

3 Preheat the oven to 70°C/150°F/gas ¼. Heat a little oil in a large, non-stick frying pan over a medium heat and spread it over the base with a crumpled piece of kitchen paper. Add 125ml/4fl oz/½ cup of the batter to the pan and tilt to coat the base. Reduce the heat to medium-low and cook for 1½–2 minutes on each side until light golden and set, then slide the pancake out of the pan on to a plate and keep warm. Repeat to make 3 more pancakes, wiping the pan with extra oil as necessary. (You may have a little batter left over; this allows for a couple of mishaps, as the first pancake doesn't always come out satisfactorily.) Cover the pancakes in foil and keep warm in the oven while you cook the stir-fry.

4 Toast the cashew nuts in a dry wok over a medium-low heat for 2–3 minutes, stirring occasionally, until light golden, then remove from the wok and set aside. Heat the sunflower oil in the wok over a high heat and stir-fry the onion for 3 minutes. Add the mangetout and carrot and stir-fry for 2 minutes. Add the Chinese leaves, garlic and ginger and stir-fry for another 1 minute, then drizzle with a little sesame oil.

5 Put 1 coconut pancake on each of four plates, top with the stir-fried vegetables and spoon the dressing over the top. Sprinkle with the cashews, coriander, basil and mint and serve.

RICE CAKES ON WILTED GREENS WITH LEMON–CHILLI BUTTER

A Mediterranean twist on fried rice cakes, this recipe brings together the flavours of chilli, thyme and feta in deliciously crisp bites.

SERVES 4

150g/5½oz/¾ cup brown basmati rice

5 spring onions, finely chopped

1 carrot, cut into fine long strips

1 long red chilli, deseeded and finely chopped

1 tbsp thyme leaves

2 eggs, lightly beaten

4 tbsp plain flour

4 tbsp double cream

85g/3oz/¾ cup feta cheese, crumbled into chunks

4 tbsp sunflower oil, for frying, plus extra as needed

salt and freshly ground black pepper

GREENS WITH LEMON–CHILLI BUTTER

300g/10½oz spring greens, shredded

1 red chilli, deseeded and thinly sliced into rounds

25g/1oz butter

1–2 tbsp lemon juice, plus lemon wedges, to serve

1 Put the rice in a saucepan and cover with cold water by about 1cm/½in. Bring to the boil, then reduce the heat to the lowest setting and simmer, covered, for 25–30 minutes until tender and the water has been absorbed. Remove from the heat and set aside, covered, for 5 minutes. Spread the rice out on a baking sheet and leave to cool completely.

2 Transfer the rice to a large bowl and mix in the spring onions, carrot, chilli, thyme, eggs, flour and cream. Season with salt and pepper and stir until combined. Gently stir in the feta, taking care not to break it up too much.

3 Preheat the oven to 70°C/150°F/gas ¼. Heat the sunflower oil in a large, non-stick frying pan over a medium heat. For each cake, pile one-quarter of the mixture in a mound in the pan, then flatten slightly with a spatula – they should be about 2cm/¾ inch thick. Reduce the heat to medium-low and cook 2 cakes at a time for 3 minutes on each side, then drain on kitchen paper. Transfer to an ovenproof plate, cover with foil and keep warm in the oven while you make the remaining 2 cakes. Add more oil to the pan, if needed.

4 Meanwhile, blanch the spring greens in boiling water for 2 minutes, then drain and return to the pan. Add the chilli and butter and toss until coated. Season with salt and pepper and stir in the lemon juice. Divide the greens on to four plates and drizzle with any buttery juices left in the pan. Top each portion with a rice cake and serve.

GYOZA IN LEMONGRASS BROTH WITH CHARGRILLED ASPARAGUS

Gyoza, also known as potstickers, are popular dumplings in Japan. Gyoza wrappers are slightly thicker than wonton wrappers (which could also be used here). You can also steam or pan-fry the gyoza.

SERVES 4

16 asparagus spears, trimmed
2 tsp sesame oil
2 tsp sunflower oil
3 tbsp chopped coriander leaves
salt and freshly ground black pepper

GYOZA

270g/9½ oz/2 cups cooked aduki beans
1 tsp sesame oil
2 tbsp light soy sauce
40g/1½ oz unpeeled root ginger, coarsely grated
3 spring onions, finely chopped
2 garlic cloves, crushed
½ tsp cornflour
55g/2oz white cabbage, finely chopped
24 gyoza wrappers, defrosted
375ml/13fl oz/1½ cups sunflower oil, for deep-frying

LEMONGRASS BROTH

1.25l/44fl oz/5 cups vegetable stock
2 lemongrass sticks, outer leaves removed, crushed
4 kaffir lime leaves
55g/2oz root ginger, peeled and thinly sliced crossways
1 tbsp vegetarian fish sauce
juice of 1 lime
½ tsp caster sugar
300ml/10½ fl oz/scant 1¼ cups coconut milk
1 long red chilli, deseeded and sliced

1 First make the gyoza. Put the aduki beans, sesame oil and half of the soy sauce in a bowl and mash lightly with the back of a fork, leaving some of the beans whole. Stir in the ginger, spring onions, garlic, cornflour and cabbage. Season with salt and pepper to taste and mix well.

2 Put 1 heaped tablespoon of the filling in the centre of a gyoza wrapper – you want the parcels to be as full as possible. Brush the edge of the wrapper with water, top with another wrapper and press the edges to seal. Set aside and repeat to make 11 more gyoza.

3 To make the lemongrass broth, put the stock, lemongrass, lime leaves, ginger, vegetarian fish sauce, lime juice and caster sugar in a large saucepan. Bring to the boil, then reduce the heat to low and simmer for 15 minutes. Strain the stock into a clean bowl, discarding the solids, and return to the saucepan. Add the remaining soy sauce, coconut milk and chilli and cook for another 5 minutes until slightly reduced and thickened. Season with salt and pepper.

4 Meanwhile, preheat the oven to 70°C/150°F/gas ¼ and heat a griddle pan over a medium heat. Toss the asparagus in the sesame and sunflower oils and griddle it for 5–7 minutes, turning occasionally, until tender and charred in places. Transfer to an ovenproof plate and keep warm in the oven.

5 To deep-fry the gyoza, heat the remaining sunflower oil in a deep saucepan to 180°C/350°F, or until a cube of bread turns golden in 40 seconds. Fry the gyoza, 3 at a time, for 2 minutes, turning once, until golden and puffed up. Remove, using a slotted spoon, and drain on kitchen paper. Transfer to an ovenproof plate and keep warm in the oven while you cook the remaining gyoza.

6 To serve, reheat the lemongrass broth, if necessary, then ladle it into four large, shallow bowls. Sprinkle with the coriander and put 3 gyoza in the centre of each bowl, slightly overlapping them. Arrange the asparagus on top and serve immediately.

BATTERED TOFU WITH CRUSHED MINT EDAMAME AND SWEET POTATO FRIES

A twist on the classic British fish and chips. Make sure the oil is heated to the correct temperature when frying the tofu to guarantee a crisp, golden batter – the same goes for the sweet potato chips, as there's nothing worse than soggy chips.

SERVES 4

100g/3½oz/heaped ¾ cup plain flour, plus extra for dusting
½ tsp salt, plus extra to serve
½ tsp hot chilli powder
1 egg, lightly beaten
100ml/3½fl oz/scant ½ cup light ale or beer
400g/14oz firm tofu, patted dry and cut into 12 x 1cm/½in thick slices
500ml/17fl oz/2 cups sunflower oil, for deep-frying
800g/1lb 12oz sweet potatoes, peeled, trimmed and cut into thick chips
freshly ground black pepper

MINT EDAMAME

250g/9oz/1⅔ cups frozen shelled edamame (soya) beans
40g/1½oz butter
1 tbsp peeled and finely grated root ginger
1 handful of chopped mint leaves
1 red chilli, deseeded and finely chopped

1 To make the batter, sift the flour, salt and chilli powder into a mixing bowl. Gradually, stir in the egg and ale to make a smooth batter, then set aside to rest for 20 minutes.

2 Preheat the oven to 70°C/150°F/gas ¼. To deep-fry the tofu, heat the sunflower oil in a wide, deep saucepan to 180°C/350°F or until a cube of bread turns golden in 40 seconds. Dust each slice of tofu in flour, dip it in the batter and carefully lower it into the hot oil. Deep-fry 4 slices at a time for 3–4 minutes or until golden and crisp, then drain on kitchen paper. Transfer to an ovenproof plate and keep warm in the oven while you repeat with the remaining tofu and batter.

3 To deep-fry the sweet potato fries, reheat the oil if necessary. Add half of the sweet potatoes and fry for 5 minutes or until crisp and golden, then drain on kitchen paper. Transfer to an ovenproof plate and keep warm in the oven while you repeat with the remaining sweet potatoes.

4 Meanwhile, boil the edamame beans for 3–5 minutes until tender. Drain, return to the pan and add the butter, ginger, mint and chilli. Heat over a medium-low heat, stirring, until the beans are coated, then lightly crush with the back of a fork.

5 Pile the sweet potatoes on to four plates and season with salt and pepper. Top with the tofu and serve immediately with the edamame beans.

UDON NOODLES WITH MANGETOUT IN SICHUAN DRESSING

The spicy, peanutty dressing in this recipe is a perfect complement to the soft and satisfying stir-fried noodles and crisp mangetout and peppers.

SERVES 4

5 spring onions
1 tbsp groundnut oil
1 large red pepper, deseeded and
    sliced into long strips
150g/5½oz mangetout
800g/1lb 12oz cooked udon noodles
1 handful of bean sprouts
a few coriander leaves
3 tbsp sunflower seeds, toasted
2 heaped tbsp broccoli sprouts

SICHUAN DRESSING

6 tbsp smooth peanut butter
150ml/5fl oz/scant ⅔ cup vegetable
    stock
2 tbsp light soy sauce
2 tsp sesame oil
1 tbsp groundnut oil
3 garlic cloves, crushed
5cm/2in piece of root ginger, peeled
    and grated
2 red chillies, deseeded and
    chopped

1 To make the Sichuan dressing, mix together the peanut butter, stock, soy sauce, sesame oil and 5 tablespoons water. Heat a large wok over a medium-high heat, add the groundnut oil and stir-fry the garlic, ginger and chillies for 1 minute. Remove the wok from the heat and stir in the peanut butter mixture, then transfer the dressing to a bowl.

2 Thinly slice 3 of the spring onions diagonally and cut the remaining spring onions into long thin strips. Wipe the wok clean and heat it over a high heat. Add the groundnut oil and stir-fry the sliced spring onions, red pepper and mangetout for 2 minutes. Remove from the wok, using a slotted spoon, and set aside.

3 Add the udon noodles and dressing to the wok and stir gently to separate and coat the noodles in the dressing. Add the stir-fried vegetables and bean sprouts and cook, stirring, for 3 minutes until warmed through.

4 Divide the udon noodles and broth into four large, shallow bowls, sprinkle with the spring onion strips, coriander leaves, sunflower seeds and broccoli sprouts and serve immediately.

WARM COURGETTE, MARJORAM AND LEMON SALAD

SERVES 4

3 tbsp extra-virgin olive oil

2 garlic cloves, thinly sliced

3 courgettes, sliced diagonally

2 tbsp marjoram or oregano leaves

2 tbsp lemon juice

salt and freshly ground black pepper

1 Heat the olive oil in a large, non-stick frying pan over a medium heat. Add the garlic and courgettes and sauté, stirring regularly, for 3 minutes until softened.

2 Reduce the heat to low, stir in the marjoram and lemon juice and season with salt and black pepper, then serve.

SESAME AND TAHINI SPINACH

SERVES 4

1 tbsp sesame seeds

1 tbsp sunflower oil

2 garlic cloves, finely chopped

400g/14oz spinach leaves, tough stalks removed

2 tbsp mirin or dry sherry

1 tbsp light tahini

2 tsp toasted sesame oil

salt and freshly ground black pepper

1 Toast the sesame seeds in a dry wok over a low heat for 5–7 minutes, stirring occasionally, until golden, then transfer to a bowl.

2 Heat the sunflower oil in the wok over a medium-low heat and fry the garlic for 30 seconds. Add the spinach and stir-fry for 2 minutes until wilted.

3 Add the mirin, tahini, sesame oil and 2 tablespoons water and toss until the spinach is coated. Season with salt and pepper to taste, sprinkle with the sesame seeds and serve.

SLOW-COOKED POTATOES

Cooking the potatoes slowly over a very low heat makes them meltingly soft and tender, with a base that's golden and slightly sticky – pure comfort food!

SERVES 4

5 saffron strands

100ml/3½ fl oz/scant ½ cup hot vegetable stock

25g/1oz butter

3 tbsp olive oil

650g/1lb 7oz potatoes, peeled and thinly sliced

4 garlic cloves, sliced

salt and freshly ground black pepper

1 Stir the saffron into the stock and leave to infuse for 5 minutes. Meanwhile, heat the butter and oil in a large, deep, non-stick frying pan over a medium-high heat and sauté the potatoes for 3–4 minutes until just starting to colour, working in batches if necessary, to avoid overcrowding the pan.

2 Arrange the potatoes in two even layers in the pan, reduce the heat to medium-low and pour the saffron stock over them. Sprinkle the garlic over the top and season with salt and pepper.

3 Bring to the boil, then reduce the heat to low. Cover snugly with a circle of baking parchment to prevent the potatoes drying out. Cover the pan with a tight-fitting lid and cook, without stirring, for 40 minutes or until the potatoes are very tender, then serve.

CAULIFLOWER AND POTATO WITH CRISP CURRY LEAVES

Potatoes, cauliflower and spices are natural partners. In this recipe, the cumin and mustard seeds and the curry leaves complement the flavour of the cauliflower especially well.

SERVES 4

2 potatoes, peeled and halved

300g/10½oz cauliflower, cut into small florets

2 tbsp sunflower oil

2 curry leaf sprigs

2 large garlic cloves, thinly sliced

2 tsp cumin seeds

2 tsp yellow mustard seeds

2 tsp fennel seeds

1 red chilli, deseeded and finely chopped

1 tsp turmeric

2 tbsp lemon juice

salt and freshly ground black pepper

1 Steam the potatoes for 12 minutes or until tender. Remove from the steamer and set aside to cool slightly, then cut into bite-sized cubes. Steam the cauliflower for 3 minutes until just tender, then refresh under cold running water and set aside.

2 Heat the sunflower oil in a large wok over a medium heat and fry the curry leaves for 2–3 minutes until crisp. Remove from the pan, using a slotted spoon, drain on kitchen paper and set aside. Add the garlic, cumin, mustard and fennel seeds and chilli to the pan and fry, stirring, for 1 minute.

3 Add the potatoes and cauliflower and turn to coat in the spice mixture. Stir in the turmeric and lemon juice, then season with salt and pepper. Top with the curry leaves and serve.

GINGER-GLAZED BRUSSELS SPROUTS AND SHALLOTS

The poor sprout has a tainted image, but when stir-fried briefly it retains its vibrant colour and crisp texture and is milder in flavour.

SERVES 4

200g/7oz small shallots, peeled

200g/7oz Brussels sprouts, peeled and trimmed

2 tbsp sunflower oil

25g/1oz butter

5cm/2in piece of root ginger, peeled and finely chopped

1 generous tbsp clear honey

salt and freshly ground black pepper

1 Blanch the shallots in boiling water for 2 minutes, then add the sprouts and cook for another 2 minutes. Drain and refresh under cold running water.

2 Heat the sunflower oil in a wok over a medium heat, add the shallots and sprouts and stir-fry for 3 minutes until softened. Reduce the heat slightly and add the butter. When it has melted, stir in the ginger and honey and season to taste with salt and pepper.

3 Stir-fry for another 1 minute until the vegetables are coated in a glossy honey glaze, then serve.

SWEET VANILLA RISOTTO CAKES WITH CARAMEL DRIZZLE

The same rules apply when making a sweet risotto as a savoury one — gradually stir in the liquid, in this case, the vanilla-infused milk, until the rice grains are creamy and tender.

SERVES 4

900ml/31fl oz/3¾ cups whole milk

1 vanilla pod, split lengthways and seeds scraped out, or 2 tsp vanilla bean paste

25g/1oz butter, plus extra for frying

200g/7oz/1 cup arborio rice

55g/2oz/¼ cup raisins (optional)

55g/2oz/scant ⅓ cup caster sugar

CARAMEL DRIZZLE

100g/3½oz/heaped ½ cup caster sugar

25g/1oz butter

6 tbsp double cream

1 Bring the milk and vanilla bean and seeds to just below the boil in a saucepan over a medium-low heat, then remove the pan from the heat and leave to stand 5 minutes to allow the vanilla to infuse the milk.

2 Melt the butter in a heavy-based saucepan over a medium-low heat, add the rice and stir for 2 minutes until the rice is coated in the butter and glossy. Remove the vanilla pod from the milk and discard. Stir in the raisins, if using, then add the milk a little at a time. Cook, stirring continuously, for 25 minutes or until all of the milk is absorbed and the rice is soft and creamy. Stir in the caster sugar and remove from the heat, then set aside to cool for 5 minutes.

3 Line a square 18cm/7in baking tin or dish with baking parchment. Transfer the risotto to the dish, spreading it out in an even layer about 2cm/¾in thick. Smooth the top with a wet palette knife, then leave to cool completely and set.

4 Turn the rice out of the tin and cut into 9 squares, using a wet knife.

5 To make the caramel drizzle, put the caster sugar and 3 tablespoons water in a deep-sided saucepan. Heat over a low heat for 3–5 minutes, stirring continuously, until it comes to the boil and the sugar dissolves. Continue to cook until the sugar turns a deep golden colour, swirling the pan occasionally rather than stirring at this stage. Remove from the heat and stir in the butter, then add the cream, taking care as it may froth up and sputter — it's a good idea to wear an oven glove. Reheat over a low heat, whisking until smooth and creamy, then set aside.

6 Preheat the oven to 70°C/150°F/gas ¼. Over a medium heat, melt enough butter to coat the base of a large non-stick frying pan. Fry half of the risotto cakes for 3 minutes on each side or until golden, reducing the heat to medium or low if necessary. Transfer the cakes to an ovenproof plate and keep warm in the oven while you cook the remaining cakes.

7 Put 2 risotto cakes on each of four plates (there will be 1 left over). Drizzle with the caramel sauce and serve.

RUM BANANAS WITH COCONUT–LIME CREAM AND WONTON CRISPS

SERVES 4

40g/1½oz butter

4 large, just-ripe bananas

2 tbsp clear honey

1 tsp ground mixed spice

4 tbsp dark rum

COCONUT AND LIME CREAM

6 tbsp full-fat natural yogurt

2 heaped tbsp coconut cream

1 tbsp icing sugar

finely grated zest of ½ lime

WONTON CRISPS

100ml/4fl oz/½ cup sunflower oil,
   for frying

4 square wonton wrappers

2 tbsp clear honey

1 tbsp sesame seeds

1 To make the wonton crisps, heat the sunflower oil in a frying pan to 170°C/325°F or until a piece of bread dropped in browns in 50 seconds. Working in batches, fry the wonton wrappers for 1 minute on each side until golden and crisp, then drain on kitchen paper. Heat the honey in a small saucepan and brush it over 1 side of each crisp. Sprinkle with the sesame seeds and set aside.

2 To make the coconut and lime cream, mix together the yogurt, coconut cream and icing sugar in a small bowl. Sprinkle the lime zest over the top and set aside.

3 Melt the butter in a large, non-stick frying pan over a medium-low heat. Peel the bananas and cut them in half lengthways, then put them in a single layer in the pan, working in batches, if necessary. Cook for 1 minute on each side, then carefully remove from the pan.

4 Add the honey, mixed spice and rum to the pan and cook for 1 minute, stirring, until the sauce starts to thicken. Return the bananas to the pan and spoon the sauce over them to coat. Cook for another 2 minutes until the fruit is tender and the sauce has become syrupy. Serve the bananas topped with the sauce, accompanied by the coconut–lime cream and wonton crisps.

ALLSPICE PAIN PERDU WITH LEMONGRASS NECTARINES

SERVES 4

2 eggs, lightly beaten

4 tbsp milk

1 tsp vanilla extract

1 tsp ground allspice

1 tbsp maple syrup, plus extra for
   drizzling

40g/1½oz butter

4 thick slices of brioche

Greek yogurt, to serve

LEMONGRASS NECTARINES

1 large lemongrass stick, crushed
   with outer leaves removed

1 tbsp caster sugar

3 slightly under-ripe nectarines,
   halved, stoned and thickly sliced

1 Preheat the oven to 70°C/150°F/gas ¼. To prepare the nectarines, put the lemongrass, caster sugar and 125ml/4fl oz/½ cup water in a saucepan and bring to the boil, stirring. Reduce the heat to low, add the nectarines and simmer for 5–7 minutes until tender. Remove from the heat and leave the nectarines to steep in the flavoured syrup. Taste and add more sugar, if necessary.

2 In a shallow dish, whisk together the eggs, milk, vanilla extract, allspice and maple syrup.

3 Melt half of the butter in a large, non-stick frying pan over a medium heat. Dunk both sides of 2 of the brioche slices into the egg mixture, then cook them for 3–4 minutes, turning once, until golden. Transfer to a plate and keep warm while you repeat with the remaining brioche.

4 Divide the pain perdu on to four plates and drizzle with a little extra maple syrup, if desired. Remove the lemongrass from the nectarines, then spoon the nectarines and a little of the lemongrass syrup alongside. Serve immediately with yogurt.

BUTTERMILK AND SOUR CHERRY PANCAKES

SERVES 4

200g/7oz/scant 1⅔ cups plain flour

a large pinch of salt

1 tsp cinnamon

1 tsp bicarbonate of soda

3 tbsp caster sugar

2 eggs, lightly beaten

290ml/10fl oz/1 cup plus 2 tbsp
   buttermilk

3 tbsp milk

100g/3½oz/heaped ¾ cup dried
   sour cherries

sunflower oil, for frying

blueberries, to serve

Greek yogurt, to serve

maple syrup or golden syrup, for
   drizzling

1 Sift the flour, salt, cinnamon, bicarbonate of soda and caster sugar into a large mixing bowl. Stir until combined, then make a well in the centre. Add the eggs, buttermilk and milk to the well and gradually work in the dry ingredients, beating to make a smooth, thick batter. Leave to rest for 20 minutes, then stir in the dried cherries.

2 Preheat the oven to 70°C/150°F/gas ¼. Heat a little oil over a medium heat in a large, non-stick frying pan, and wipe away any excess with a crumpled piece of kitchen paper. Drop 3 spoonfuls of the batter into the pan, spacing them apart. Reduce the heat to medium-low and cook for 2–3 minutes or until bubbles appear on the surface, then flip over and cook for another 2 minutes. Transfer to an ovenproof plate and keep warm in the oven while you cook the remaining pancakes.

3 Allow 3 pancakes per person. Top with blueberries and a generous spoonful of yogurt, then drizzle with maple syrup and serve.

BANANA AND APPLE SESAME FRITTERS

SERVES 4

100g/3½oz/heaped ¾ cup plain
   flour

a large pinch of salt

5 tbsp milk

500ml/17fl oz/2 cups sunflower oil

2 egg whites

2 tbsp sesame seeds

3 bananas

2 apples

1 tbsp lemon juice

caster sugar, for dusting

1 Sift the flour and salt into a mixing bowl. Make a well in the centre, add the milk, 1 tablespoon of the sunflower oil and 5 tablespoons water to the well and gradually work in the flour, beating to make a thick, smooth batter. Leave to rest for 20 minutes.

2 Preheat the oven to 70°C/150°F/gas ¼. Whisk the egg whites in a separate clean bowl until they form soft peaks, then fold them into the batter in two batches. Stir in the sesame seeds.

3 Peel the bananas, halve them crossways and then cut in half again lengthways. Peel the apples (there is no need to core them) then cut into 5mm/¼in slices, discarding any seeds. Brush bananas and apples with lemon juice to prevent them browning.

4 To deep-fry the fritters, heat the remaining oil in a wide, deep saucepan to 180°C/350°F, or until a piece of bread turns golden in 40 seconds. Dunk the banana slices into the batter, one at a time, and fry 5 pieces at a time for 2–3 minutes until golden. Using a slotted spoon, remove the fritters and drain on kitchen paper. Transfer to an ovenproof plate and keep warm in the oven while you fry the remaining banana fritters. Pat the apple slices dry with kitchen paper and fry in the same way. When all the fritters are cooked, sprinkle them with caster sugar and serve immediately.

CINNAMON-DUSTED DOUGHNUTS WITH CHOCOLATE SAUCE

These light and fluffy doughnuts are infused with orange zest and are best eaten warm, soon after cooking – perfect dunked into the rich chocolate sauce.

SERVES 4-6

100ml/3½fl oz/scant ½ cup single cream

1 large egg, lightly beaten

60g/2¼oz/heaped ¼ cup caster sugar

100ml/3½fl oz/scant ½ cup freshly squeezed orange juice

finely grated zest of 1 orange

3 tbsp olive oil

425g/15oz/scant 3½ cups self-raising flour, plus extra for kneading

500ml/17fl oz/2 cups sunflower oil, for deep frying

CINNAMON DUST

5 tbsp caster sugar

1 tsp cinnamon

CHOCOLATE SAUCE

200ml/7fl oz/scant 1 cup milk

50g/1¾oz dark chocolate, broken into small chunks

2 tsp cornflour

40g/1½oz/scant ¼ cup caster sugar

1 In a large mixing bowl, whisk the cream, egg, caster sugar, orange juice, orange zest and olive oil until combined. Sift in the flour and mix to make a soft dough.

2 Turn out the dough and knead it on a lightly floured work surface for 1 minute to form a soft ball of dough. Using floured hands, divide the dough into 16 pieces. Roll out each piece with your hands into a sausage shape, about 15cm/6in long, then press the ends together to form a ring. Run your finger around the inside to make a hole, then transfer to a lightly floured plate.

3 To make the cinnamon dust, mix together the caster sugar and cinnamon on a plate and set aside. To make the chocolate sauce, put half of the milk in a saucepan over a medium heat and bring to just below the boil. Reduce the heat to low, add the chocolate and stir until melted. Mix together the remaining milk, cornflour and caster sugar in a bowl and add it to the chocolate milk mixture. Stir over a medium-low heat for 3–5 minutes until thickened, then transfer to a serving bowl.

4 Preheat the oven to 70°C/150°F/gas ¼ and heat the sunflower oil in a wide, deep saucepan to 180°C/350°F, or until a piece of bread turns golden after 40 seconds. Fry the doughnuts, 3 at a time, for about 4 minutes, turning once, until golden. Remove with a slotted spoon and drain on kitchen paper, then transfer to an ovenproof plate and keep warm in the oven while you cook the remaining doughnuts.

5 Roll the doughnuts in the cinnamon dust until lightly coated. Serve warm with the chocolate sauce.

Gentle and healthy, steaming is perfect for cooking delicate ingredients and retaining precious nutrients. Surprisingly versatile, it's ideal for cooking vegetables quickly to create clean, fresh flavours and keep their crisp texture, as well as slow-cooking dishes, such as the ultimate comfort food – puddings.

STEAM

Crushed Pea and Ginger Wontons, page 129

SPRING VEGETABLES WITH CRUNCHY WALNUT CRUMBLE

I love the contrast in texture and colour in this dish, from the crunchy, garlicky, nutty crumbs to the steamed delicate freshness of the spring vegetables.

SERVES 4

100g/3½ oz shelled broad beans
200g/7oz baby carrots, trimmed
150g/5½ oz fine green beans
150g/5½ oz asparagus, trimmed
150g/5½ oz baby courgettes,
   halved lengthways
1 tbsp olive oil
1 tbsp lemon juice
½ tsp Dijon mustard
sea salt and freshly ground black
   pepper

WALNUT CRUMBLE

70g/2½ oz/scant ⅔ cup walnut
   halves
1 tbsp olive oil
25g/1oz butter
70g/2½ oz/1¼ cups fresh white
   breadcrumbs
1 large garlic clove, finely chopped
1 red chilli, deseeded and chopped

HARISSA MAYONNAISE

125ml/4fl oz/½ cup mayonnaise
1 garlic clove, very finely chopped
1 tsp harissa paste

1 To make the harissa mayonnaise, mix together the mayonnaise, garlic and harissa and set aside.

2 To make the walnut crumble, toast the walnuts in a dry frying pan over a medium heat for 4–5 minutes, stirring occasionally, until light golden, then chop coarsely and set aside. Heat the olive oil and butter in a frying pan over a medium-high heat and fry the breadcrumbs for 3 minutes, stirring often, until crisp and light golden. Add the garlic and chilli and cook, stirring, for another 2 minutes. Remove from the heat and stir in the walnuts.

3 Steam the broad beans for 3 minutes, then, when cool enough to handle, pop them out of their outer shells to reveal the bright green bean inside. Keep them warm while you steam the carrots and green beans for 5 minutes or until tender. Again, keep the vegetables warm while you steam the asparagus and courgettes for 3 minutes or until tender.

4 Meanwhile, mix together the olive oil, lemon juice and mustard and season with salt and pepper. Pour this dressing over the warm vegetables, sprinkle the walnut crumble over the top and serve with the harissa mayonnaise.

WARM BROCCOLI, MOZZARELLA AND CHILLI SALAD

SERVES 4

400g/14oz long-stemmed broccoli, trimmed

4 tbsp olive oil

2 large garlic cloves, thinly sliced

1 long red chilli, deseeded and thinly sliced

2 tbsp small capers, rinsed and drained

4 tbsp lemon juice

250g/9oz mozzarella cheese, preferably buffalo, drained

salt and freshly ground black pepper

a few basil leaves, to serve

1 Steam the broccoli for 3–4 minutes or until tender.

2 Meanwhile, heat the oil in a pan over a medium-low heat and fry the garlic, chilli and capers for 1 minute, stirring often. Add the lemon juice and season with salt and pepper.

3 Put the warm broccoli on a serving plate. Tear the mozzarella into chunks and sprinkle it over the top. Pour the garlic mixture over the broccoli and mozzarella, sprinkle with the basil leaves and serve.

JAPANESE SOBA NOODLE SALAD WITH SESAME–TOFU DRESSING

Spicy togarashi seasoning adds a fragrant kick to this salad. You can make the noodles and vegetables ahead of time, simply refresh them under cold running water and store in airtight containers until ready to use.

SERVES 4

250g/9oz soba noodles

2 tbsp sesame seeds

2 carrots, thinly sliced into ribbons

2 leeks, halved crossways and sliced lengthways into thin strips

165g/5¾ oz mangetout

200g/7oz asparagus tips, trimmed

2 tbsp thinly sliced chives

½ tsp togarashi seasoning (optional)

SESAME–TOFU DRESSING

70g/2½ oz silken tofu

1 tbsp tamari soy sauce

2 tbsp mirin

2 tsp peeled and finely grated root ginger

1 tsp caster sugar

salt and freshly ground black pepper

1 Cook the noodles in plenty of boiling salted water following the packet instructions, then drain.

2 Meanwhile, toast the sesame seeds in a dry frying pan over a medium-low heat, stirring occasionally, for 3–5 minutes until light golden, then set aside. Steam the carrots, leeks, mangetout and asparagus for 3 minutes or until tender.

3 To make the dressing, blend together the tofu, tamari, mirin, ginger and sugar, adding 1 tablespoon of the toasted sesame seeds, and season with salt and pepper.

4 Toss the noodles with half of the dressing, then divide on to four plates. Top with the vegetables and drizzle with the remaining dressing. Sprinkle with the remaining sesame seeds, chives and togarashi seasoning and serve warm or at room temperature.

CHINESE RICE IN BEANCURD POCKETS

Abura-age is a Japanese deep-fried tofu (beancurd) parcel available from oriental speciality shops. Normally sold frozen, they defrost in minutes and can then be split open and stuffed. Here, they are filled with a mixture of vegetables and herbs and served with a chilli and hoisin dipping sauce.

SERVES 4

15g/½ oz dried shiitake mushrooms
1 large carrot, grated
4 spring onions, thinly sliced
150g/5½ oz Chinese leaves, shredded
2 garlic cloves, crushed
4 water chestnuts, finely chopped
2 tbsp chopped coriander leaves, plus extra to serve
1 tbsp light soy sauce
1 tbsp peeled and finely grated root ginger
6 deep-fried tofu parcels (abura-age), defrosted if frozen

DIPPING SAUCE

4 tbsp sweet chilli sauce
2 tbsp light soy sauce
2 tbsp hoisin sauce
2 tbsp crushed unsalted peanuts

1. Soak the shiitake mushrooms in hot water for 20 minutes until softened. Drain, squeeze out any excess water and finely chop.
2. Meanwhile, make the dipping sauce. In a small bowl, mix together all of the ingredients for the sauce and 1 tablespoon water, then set aside.
3. In another bowl, mix together the shiitake mushrooms, carrot, spring onions, Chinese leaves, garlic, water chestnuts, coriander leaves, soy sauce and ginger.
4. Cut the tofu parcels in half crossways and open each one out to make a pocket. Stuff with the vegetable mixture and stand the pockets upright in a steamer lined with baking parchment. (Use a tiered steamer if you have one or steam the pockets in two batches, keeping them warm as needed.) Cover and steam for 6–8 minutes, or until the vegetables are tender.
5. Sprinkle the stuffed beancurd pockets with extra coriander and serve with the dipping sauce on the side, allowing 3 pockets per person.

CRUSHED PEA AND GINGER WONTONS

Vibrant in colour and packed with oriental flavours, these pea dumplings make a perfect light lunch accompanied by miso soup, or an elegant starter. Choose wonton wrappers specifically for steaming, and if you don't have a bamboo steamer, use a regular one.

MAKES 32 (SERVES 4–6)
250g/9oz/1⅔ cups frozen peas
3 spring onions, finely chopped
4cm/1½ in piece of root ginger,
 peeled and very finely chopped
1 tsp soy sauce, plus extra to serve
32 wonton wrappers, defrosted if
 frozen
1 small red chilli, deseeded and
 finely sliced (optional)
a few chives, finely chopped,
 to serve
freshly ground black pepper

1 Steam the peas for 3 minutes or until tender, then drain, if necessary, and transfer to a mixing bowl. Mash with a potato masher or the back of a fork until crushed but not completely smooth. Stir in the spring onions, ginger and soy sauce, then season with pepper.

2 Put 1 wonton wrapper on a plate, keeping the others covered with a clean, damp tea towel. Put 1 heaped teaspoon of the pea mixture in the centre and brush the edges of the wrapper with water. Gather up the sides around the filling and pinch together at the top to seal – it should look similar to a money-bag. Set the dumpling aside, covered with another clean, damp tea towel, and repeat with the remaining wonton wrappers and filling.

3 Put 8 of the dumplings in a large bamboo steamer lined with baking parchment. Cover and steam over a wok of simmering water for 8 minutes until the wonton wrappers are cooked and slightly translucent. Transfer the cooked dumplings to a plate and cover to keep warm while you steam the remaining dumplings. If necessary, occasionally replenish the water in the wok to prevent it from drying out during steaming.

4 To serve, pour a little soy sauce in four or six small dishes (one per person), then divide the chilli, if using, among them. Sprinkle the dumplings with chives and serve warm with the dipping sauce.

SUSHI BOWL WITH WASABI CASHEWS

SERVES 4

300g/10½oz/1½ cups sushi rice

2 tbsp ume plum seasoning or rice vinegar

4 tbsp freshly squeezed orange juice

1 tbsp sesame oil, plus extra for dressing the vegetables

2 tbsp light soy sauce, plus extra for dressing the vegetables

100g/3½oz green beans, trimmed and thinly sliced on the diagonal

100g/3½oz/¾ cup shelled edamame beans

1 large carrot, cut into fine strips

4 tsp sesame seeds, toasted

1 quarter nori sheet, cut into fine strips

20g/¾oz pink pickled ginger, to serve

JAPANESE OMELETTE

2 large eggs, plus 1 large egg yolk

1 tsp light soy sauce

1 tsp caster sugar

sunflower oil, for frying

WASABI CASHEWS

80g/2¾oz/½ cup cashew nuts

1 tbsp caster sugar

1 heaped tbsp wasabi paste

a generous pinch of salt

1 Preheat the oven to 110°C/225°F/gas ½. To make the wasabi cashews, toast the cashew nuts in a dry frying pan over a medium heat for 5 minutes, stirring occasionally, until light golden, then set aside. Put the sugar and 1 tablespoon water in a small pan, bring to the boil, reduce the heat and stir until dissolved. Remove the pan from the heat, stir in the wasabi and salt, then add the cashews. Stir until the cashews are coated in the wasabi mixture. Transfer to a baking tray lined with baking parchment and roast for 35–40 minutes until crunchy, then set aside. They might still be a little sticky when they some out of the oven, but will dry when cooled.

2 Wash the rice in several changes of water, then drain and transfer to a heavy-based saucepan. Add enough water to cover the rice by 1cm/½in and bring to the boil. Reduce the heat to low, stir, cover with a tight-fitting lid and simmer for 10–12 minutes until the water is absorbed. Remove from the heat and leave to stand, covered, for 10 minutes. Meanwhile, mix together the ume plum seasoning, orange juice, sesame oil and soy sauce to make a dressing for the rice.

3 Transfer the hot rice to a bowl and carefully fold in the dressing – do not stir. Cover with a plate and set aside.

4 To make the Japanese omelette, lightly whisk together the eggs, yolk, soy sauce, caster sugar and 2 tablespoons water in a bowl. Heat a large, non-stick frying pan over a medium-low heat, add a little sunflower oil and wipe away any excess using kitchen towel. Add the egg mixture and swirl it around the pan. Cook for 3–5 minutes or until half set. Fold it in half, then fold in the two sides to make a parcel. Turn the omelette over, cook briefly, then slide it out of the pan and cut into thin strips.

5 Meanwhile, steam the green beans for 2 minutes. Add the edamame and carrots and steam for another 2–3 minutes until tender. Transfer to a bowl and toss with a little sesame oil and soy sauce, to taste. Sprinkle with the sesame seeds.

6 To serve, spoon a quarter of the rice into a small bowl and press down to level the top, then turn it out on to a serving plate. Repeat with the remaining rice. Top each portion of rice with the nori, egg and wasabi cashews and serve with the vegetables and pickled ginger alongside. You can also present this dish in a more relaxed way, with the vegetables and omelette mixed casually into the rice.

CREAMY LEEK AND CHEESE ROULADES

SERVES 4

300g/10½oz/scant 2½ cups
    self-raising flour, plus extra for
    kneading
2 tsp baking powder
1 tsp vegetable bouillon powder
1 tsp English mustard powder
a generous pinch of salt, plus extra
    to season
85g/3oz butter
2 tbsp chopped chives
1 large egg, lightly beaten
85–100ml/2¾–3½fl oz/⅓–scant
    ½ cup milk
freshly ground black pepper
1 recipe quantity Watercress Sauce
    (see page 67)

FILLING

1 tbsp olive oil
1 onion, finely chopped
2 leeks, finely chopped
1 tbsp thyme leaves
2 tbsp crème fraîche
2 tsp Dijon mustard
70g/2½oz/heaped ½ cup grated
    mature Cheddar cheese

1 Sift the flour, baking powder, bouillon powder, mustard powder and salt into a mixing bowl. Rub in the butter until the mixture resembles coarse crumbs, then stir in the chives, egg and 85ml/2¾fl oz/⅓ cup of the milk. Bring the dough together with your hands and knead lightly on a lightly floured surface to make a soft ball of dough, adding a little extra milk if it's too dry. Set aside, wrapped in cling film, while you prepare the filling.

2 Heat the olive oil in a frying pan over a medium-low heat. Add the onion and leeks, cover and cook for 5 minutes, stirring occasionally, until soft. Remove the pan from the heat and stir in the thyme, crème fraîche, mustard and cheese. Season with salt and pepper.

3 Divide the dough into 4 equal pieces. On a lightly floured surface, roll each one out into a rectangle about 14 x 13cm/5½ x 5in. Spoon a quarter of the leek mixture down the middle of each rectangle and roll into a large log, enclosing the filling. Wet the edge and ends then press gently to seal. Prick the top three times and roll each roulade in greaseproof paper, twisting the ends of the paper closed.

4 Put the parcels in a large steamer and steam for 18–20 minutes until risen and cooked through – they will look like long suet dumplings. Unwrap and slice each roulade in half diagonally. Serve with the watercress sauce.

THAI TOFU AND VEGETABLES IN BANANA LEAVES

Banana leaves make attractive parcels and are available at Asian food shops, but if you can't find them, use baking parchment. Serve these parcels with Thai jasmine rice.

SERVES 4

4 small banana leaves

2 blocks of firm tofu, each about 250g/9oz

5cm/2in piece of root ginger, peeled and grated

2 small red chillies, deseeded and finely chopped

2 lemongrass sticks, finely chopped, with outer leaves removed

2 tbsp vegetarian fish sauce

2 tbsp light soy sauce

juice of 1 lime

1 tsp soft light brown sugar

2 tbsp sesame seeds, toasted

175g/6oz sugar snap peas

1 red pepper, deseeded and thinly sliced

1 carrot, cut into ribbons

8 kaffir lime leaves

4 spring onions, sliced

4 tbsp chopped coriander leaves, plus extra to serve

1 Soak the banana leaves for a few minutes in warm water until pliable. Slice each tofu block into 4 pieces.

2 Mix together the ginger, chillies, lemongrass, fish sauce, soy sauce, lime juice, brown sugar and sesame seeds in a bowl.

3 Spread the banana leaves out on a work surface and divide the peas, red pepper and carrot in the centre of the leaves. Top each portion with 2 slices of the tofu. Spoon the ginger mixture over the top and top each portion with 2 kaffir lime leaves. Sprinkle with the spring onions and coriander.

4 Fold in the sides of each banana leaf and roll up to make a parcel. Secure each parcel with a piece of string and steam in a two-tier bamboo steamer, or in batches in a regular steamer, for 8 minutes.

5 Put each parcel on a serving plate and open carefully. Sprinkle with extra coriander leaves and serve.

ORANGE AND SQUASH TABBOULEH WITH HERB FETA

SERVES 4

70g/2½oz/heaped ½ cup raisins
125ml/4fl oz/½ cup orange juice
225g/8oz/1¼ cups bulgur wheat
1 tsp vegetable bouillon powder
2 tbsp olive oil
750g/1lb 10oz butternut squash,
   peeled, deseeded and cut into
   bite-sized pieces
1 large onion, chopped
2 large garlic cloves, chopped
zest of 1 large orange
1 tbsp ground sumac
1 large handful of coriander leaves,
   chopped, plus extra to serve
salt and freshly ground black pepper

BAKED FETA

2 blocks of feta cheese, each about
   200g/7oz, drained
2 tbsp olive oil
2 tbsp lemon thyme leaves

1 Soak the raisins in the orange juice for about 30 minutes until softened. Meanwhile, make the baked feta. Preheat the oven to 180°C/350°F/gas 4 and put each block of feta on a large piece of foil and sprinkle each one with half of the olive oil and half of the thyme. Season with pepper, then fold the foil over and seal to make two parcels. Bake on a baking sheet for 15 minutes until softened.

2 While the feta is baking, put the bulgur wheat in a heatproof bowl and cover with boiled water. Stir in the bouillon powder and set aside for 5 minutes, then drain and transfer to a steamer basket lined with muslin or cheesecloth. Steam for 10 minutes until tender, then set aside.

3 Heat the olive oil in a large frying pan over a medium-low heat and fry the squash for 10–15 minutes, stirring occasionally, until tender and golden. Remove from the pan, using a slotted spoon. Add the onion, fry for 5 minutes, then stir in the garlic, orange zest and sumac. Mix in the bulgur, squash, orange juice and raisins and warm through. Season with salt and pepper and stir in the coriander.

4 Divide the tabbouleh on to four plates. Open the feta parcels and cut each block of feta in half. Top each portion of tabbouleh with a piece of feta, sprinkle with extra coriander and serve.

SOY-STEAMED TOFU WITH THAI BASIL

SERVES 4

2 tbsp tamari soy sauce
6 tbsp kecap manis
2 tbsp sesame oil
500g/1lb 2oz firm tofu, patted dry
   and cut into wedges
4 tbsp olive oil
1 long red chilli, deseeded and thinly
   sliced lengthways
4cm/1½in piece of root ginger,
   peeled and thinly sliced into
   strips
3 spring onions, shredded
a few Thai basil leaves

1 In a shallow dish, mix together the tamari, kecap manis and sesame oil. Add the tofu and spoon the marinade over it until coated. Leave to marinate for at least 30 minutes.

2 Meanwhile, heat the olive oil in a small frying pan over a medium heat and fry the chilli and ginger, stirring occasionally, until crisp. Drain on kitchen paper and set aside.

3 Remove the tofu from the marinade, using a spatula, and reserve the marinade. Put the tofu in a large steamer lined with baking parchment and steam for 5 minutes.

4 Heat the reserved marinade in a small pan until warm. Carefully remove the tofu from the steamer and transfer to four plates. Spoon the marinade over the tofu, top with the spring onions, basil and crispy chilli and ginger, then serve.

MUSHROOM, CHESTNUT AND PRUNE PUDDINGS

Suet pastry, a traditional British classic, is at its best when freshly cooked (by steaming or boiling). Covering the puddings with pleated baking parchment and foil allows room for expansion during steaming.

SERVES 4

2 tbsp olive oil, plus extra for greasing
1 large onion, chopped
1 large garlic clove, crushed
250g/9oz portobello mushrooms, coarsely chopped
110g/3¾ oz cooked chestnuts, chopped
1 tsp dried thyme
60g/2¼ oz ready-to-eat prunes, chopped
300ml/10½ fl oz/scant 1¼ cups dry red wine
1 tbsp soy sauce
a few drops of hot-pepper sauce
salt and freshly ground black pepper

VEGETABLE SUET PASTRY

200g/7oz/scant 1⅔ cups self-raising flour, plus extra for kneading
a pinch of salt
100g/3½ oz shredded vegetable suet

RED WINE JUS

200ml/7fl oz/scant 1 cup dry red wine
200ml/7fl oz/scant 1 cup vegetable stock
1 tbsp balsamic vinegar
1 tsp caster sugar
25g/1oz butter

1 Lightly grease four 250ml/9fl oz/1 cup pudding basins with a little olive oil. Heat the oil in a large frying pan over a medium-low heat and cook the onion for 8 minutes until softened. Add the garlic and mushrooms and cook for 4 minutes, stirring often. Add the chestnuts, thyme, prunes and wine and bring to the boil, then reduce the heat to low and simmer for 5–8 minutes until reduced and there is no aroma of alcohol. Stir in the soy sauce and hot-pepper sauce, heat through and season with salt and pepper, then leave to cool.

2 To make the pastry, sift the flour and salt into a mixing bowl. Stir in the suet, add 125ml/4fl oz/½ cup water and mix to form a smooth, soft dough. Reserve a quarter of the dough and roll out the remainder on a lightly floured surface to about 3mm/⅛ in thick. Cut out 4 circles large enough to line each pudding basin and leave a little overhang. Spoon the cooled mushroom mixture into the pastry-lined basins.

3 Roll out the remaining pastry and cut out 4 circles to cover the top of the puddings. Dampen the edges of the pastry with water and lay the circles over the puddings. Press to seal, then trim any excess.

4 Cover each pudding with a piece of baking parchment, then a round of foil (both with a pleat down the centre) and secure with string. Put the puddings in a large tiered steamer, cover and steam for 45 minutes and carefully remove the puddings from the pan. (Check the water in the pan occasionally to make sure it is not running dry.) Run a knife around the edge of the puddings before turning them out.

5 While the puddings are cooking, make the red wine jus. Heat the red wine in a frying pan until boiling, then reduce the heat to medium-low and cook for 10 minutes until reduced by half. Add the stock, vinegar and sugar and cook for another 5 minutes until thickened slightly. Remove from the heat, stir in the butter to make a glossy sauce and season with salt and pepper. Serve with the puddings.

STUFFED SAVOY CABBAGE WITH CAULIFLOWER CREAM

Blanching the cabbage leaves first makes them flexible and easier to fold after filling with the spicy potato and chickpea mixture.

SERVES 4

225g/8oz potatoes, peeled and
    quartered, if large
8 large savoy cabbage leaves
2 tbsp olive oil
1 large onion, finely chopped
1 large garlic clove, chopped
1 heaped tbsp peeled and chopped
    root ginger
1 tsp fenugreek seeds
2 tsp ground cumin
1 tsp ground coriander
½ tsp hot chilli powder
1 tbsp tamarind paste
140g/5oz/1 cup cooked chickpeas,
    roughly mashed
1 carrot, grated
salt and freshly ground black pepper

CAULIFLOWER CREAM

350g/12oz cauliflower florets
2 tbsp olive oil
2 shallots, finely chopped
2 garlic cloves, chopped
250ml/9fl oz/1 cup vegetable stock
3 tbsp crème fraîche

1 Cook the potatoes in boiling salted water for 10–12 minutes until tender. Drain, cut into small dice and transfer to a large bowl.

2 Meanwhile, steam the cauliflower for 4 minutes or until tender, then set aside. Bring a large saucepan of water to the boil. Cut a small v-shaped piece from the base of the stem of each cabbage leaf to make them easier to fold. Blanch the leaves for 1 minute or until flexible enough to allow folding without breaking. Drain and refresh under cold running water.

3 Heat the olive oil in a frying pan over a medium-low heat and fry the onion for 8 minutes until softened. Add the garlic, ginger, fenugreek, cumin, coriander and chilli powder and cook for 1 minute. Stir in the tamarind paste and 2 tablespoons water and heat through, then add the mixture to the potato. Add the chickpeas and carrot, mix well and season well with salt and pepper.

4 Put 2 tablespoons of the potato mixture in the centre of each cabbage leaf. Fold the sides of each leaf over the filling, then roll up from the bottom to make 8 parcels.

5 Put the bundles, seam-side down, in a two-tiered steamer, cover and steam for 6 minutes until heated through. Or line a large steamer with baking parchment, cover and steam the bundles in two batches, then cover and keep warm while you cook the second batch.

6 To finish the cauliflower cream, heat the olive oil in a large sauté pan and sauté the shallots for 5 minutes until softened. Add the garlic and cook for 1 minute, then transfer to a blender. Add the cauliflower, stock and crème fraîche and blend until smooth. Reheat gently in the pan and season with salt and pepper.

7 To serve, divide the cauliflower cream on to four plates. Top each portion with 2 savoy cabbage parcels and season with black pepper.

CREAMY PEA PURÉE

SERVES 4

250g/9oz/scant 2 cups fresh or
    frozen petit pois
2 tbsp crème fraîche
1 tbsp olive oil
2 tbsp chopped mint leaves, plus
    extra to serve
1 tsp lemon juice
salt and freshly ground black pepper

1 Steam the peas for 3 minutes or until tender, then transfer them to
   a blender.
2 Add the crème fraîche, olive oil, mint, lemon juice and 2 tablespoons
   hot water and blend until puréed. Season with salt and pepper,
   sprinkle with extra mint leaves and serve warm.

ARTICHOKES WITH LEMON AND GARLIC MAYO

When in season, artichokes are best eaten simply steamed with butter or
mayonnaise. Always use a stainless steel knife and pan when preparing and
cooking artichokes since iron and aluminium, including foil, will discolour them.
The mayonnaise is made by hand but can also be done in a food processor; it will
keep for up to 5 days in the fridge.

SERVES 4

juice of ½ lemon
4 globe artichokes, rinsed

LEMON AND GARLIC MAYONNAISE
1 egg yolk, at room temperature
½ tsp English mustard powder
100ml/3 ½ fl oz/scant ½ cup
    sunflower oil
1 tsp white wine vinegar
1 garlic clove, crushed
finely grated zest of ½ lemon
salt and freshly ground black pepper

1 First make the mayonnaise. In a mixing bowl, whisk together the
   egg yolk and mustard powder. Season with salt and pepper, then
   gradually whisk in the sunflower oil, adding just a few drops at
   first and whisking until thoroughly incorporated. After a while,
   you can add a greater quantity at a time, but make sure it is well
   incorporated before adding more. Once all the oil is mixed in and the
   mixture has emulsified and thickened, stir in the vinegar, garlic and
   lemon zest. Cover and chill in the fridge until ready to use.
2 To prepare the artichokes, fill a bowl with water and mix in the
   lemon juice. Remove the tough outer leaves and cut off the stem
   from each artichoke, taking care not to cut into the base. Cut off
   the top 1cm/½ in and then, using a pair of scissors, trim the outer
   leaves. Dip the artichoke in the acidulated water to stop them from
   discolouring. Repeat with the rest of the artichokes.
3 Fill the steamer pan with about 5cm/2in water and bring to the
   boil. Put the artichokes in a single layer, stem-side down, in the
   steamer basket, cover and steam for 20–35 minutes, depending
   on their size, until tender. The artichokes are done when the leaves
   pull away easily. Remove the artichokes with tongs and drain
   upside down in a colander. Serve warm or at room temperature
   with the mayonnaise.

CUMIN-SPIKED AUBERGINE

Aubergines are renowned for soaking up large quantities of oil during cooking, but steaming them helps to prevent this and, surprisingly, they become meltingly tender when cooked this way.

SERVES 4

2 tsp cumin seeds
3 tbsp olive oil
½ tsp dried chilli flakes
4 tomatoes, deseeded and diced
400ml/14fl oz/scant 1⅔ cups
    tinned chopped tomatoes
juice of ½ lemon
2 tbsp capers, drained and rinsed
1 handful of coriander leaves,
    chopped
1 aubergine, peeled and cut into
    large chunks
2 large garlic cloves, peeled
salt and freshly ground black pepper

1 Toast the cumin seeds in a dry frying pan over a medium heat for 2–3 minutes, stirring occasionally, until lightly browned. Then remove from the heat and set aside.
2 Heat the olive oil in a sauté pan, add the cumin seeds and toast, stirring occasionally for 1–2 minutes or until they smell aromatic. Watch carefully so they do not burn. Add the chilli flakes and the fresh and tinned tomatoes and simmer, stirring occasionally, for 10 minutes until reduced and thickened. Stir in the lemon juice and capers, season with salt and pepper and stir in the coriander.
3 Meanwhile, put the aubergine and garlic in a steamer basket, cover and steam for 5–7 minutes until very tender, then lightly mash with a fork – the mixture should still be quite chunky. Stir the aubergine and garlic into the tomato sauce and serve.

GINGER AND MANGO COUSCOUS

SERVES 4

175g/6oz/scant 1 cup wholemeal
    couscous
3 tbsp olive oil
juice of 1 lemon
1 garlic clove, crushed
1 tbsp peeled and finely grated root
    ginger
1 long red chilli, deseeded and finely
    chopped
1 handful of coriander leaves,
    chopped
1 handful of mint leaves, chopped
1 handful of flat-leaf parsley leaves,
    chopped
1 mango, peeled, stoned and diced
salt and freshly ground black pepper

1 Put the couscous in a bowl, cover with boiling water and leave to soak for 3 minutes, then drain. Transfer to a steamer lined with muslin or cheesecloth, cover and steam for 3 minutes until the grains are tender and fluffy. Transfer the couscous to a serving bowl.
2 Drizzle the olive oil and lemon juice over the couscous and add the garlic, ginger, chilli, coriander, mint and parsley. Stir until combined, then season with salt and pepper.
3 Stir the mango into the couscous and serve at room temperature.

WARM GREEN BEAN SALAD

Dress the green beans while they're still warm and they will absorb the flavour of the oriental dressing more readily.

SERVES 4

250g/9oz fine green beans, trimmed
4 tbsp sunflower oil
2 large garlic cloves, thinly sliced
5cm/2in piece of root ginger, peeled and grated
1 tbsp sesame oil
salt and freshly ground black pepper

1 Steam the green beans for 5 minutes or until tender, then arrange on a serving plate.
2 Meanwhile, heat the sunflower oil in a wok over a medium-low heat. Add the garlic and stir-fry for 2 minutes, or until light golden and starting to crisp. Remove from the wok with a slotted spoon and drain on kitchen paper.
3 Put the ginger in the centre of a piece of kitchen towel. Twist it into a bundle and squeeze to release the juices into a bowl. Add the sesame oil, season with salt and pepper and pour the dressing over the green beans. Sprinkle with the garlic, then serve warm or at room temperature.

LEMONGRASS AND GINGER RICE

This fragrant rice dish cooks for a short time in water and is then finished by the steam trapped inside the pan. Make sure the lid on the pan fits snuggly, or wrap the lid in a clean dry tea towel to help trap the steam in the pan.

SERVES 4

325g/11½oz/1½ cups basmati rice
2 lemongrass sticks, crushed, with outer leaves removed
3 kaffir lime leaves
2 tbsp sesame seeds
1 tbsp sunflower oil
2 large garlic cloves, sliced
7cm/2¾in piece root ginger, peeled and cut into matchsticks
2 tbsp light soy sauce
2 tsp sesame oil

1 Put the rice and 750ml/26fl oz/3 cups water in a saucepan. Stir in the lemongrass and kaffir lime leaves and bring to the boil. Reduce the heat to low, cover with a tight-fitting lid and simmer for 10–12 minutes until the water is absorbed and the rice is tender. Do not remove the lid during the cooking or the steam will escape. Remove the pan from the heat and leave to stand for 5–10 minutes.
2 Meanwhile, toast the sesame seeds in a dry frying pan over a medium heat for 3–4 minutes, stirring occasionally, until lightly browned. Then remove from the heat and set aside.
3 Fluff up the rice with a fork. Heat the sunflower oil in a pan over a medium-low heat and fry the garlic and ginger for 1 minute. Add the soy sauce and sesame oil, then stir the mixture into the rice. Sprinkle the sesame seeds over the rice and serve.

MANGO SUSHI

Fresh mango steeped in a ginger sugar syrup provides a sweet contrast to the sticky coconut rice. A wet knife makes the rice easier to cut and gives this dish a neater, more stylized presentation.

MAKES 16 PIECES

100g/3½oz/scant ½ cup sushi rice, rinsed

150ml/5fl oz/scant ⅔ cup coconut milk

½ tsp freshly grated nutmeg

6 tbsp caster sugar

1 mango

4cm/1½ in piece of root ginger, peeled and thinly sliced

1 Put the rice in a saucepan and add enough water to just cover it. Bring to the boil and cook for 3 minutes until beginning to soften, then drain well. Put the rice in a steamer lined with muslin or cheesecloth, cover and steam for 12−15 minutes until tender.

2 Carefully lift out the muslin and transfer the rice to a heavy-based saucepan. Add the coconut milk, nutmeg and 2 tablespoons of the caster sugar and stir until combined. Bring to the boil, then reduce the heat to low and simmer for 6 minutes until thick and creamy, stirring regularly to prevent the rice from sticking.

3 Line a small baking dish, about 18 x 25cm/7 x 10in, with cling film, leaving enough overhanging the sides to cover the top when folded over. Spread the rice out to about 2cm/¾in thick and smooth the top with a wet palette knife. Fold the overhanging cling film over the top to cover and then leave to cool.

4 Peel the mango and slice thinly, discarding the stone. Cut the slices into 16 pieces, each 4 x 2cm/1½ x ¾in. Put the remaining caster sugar and 125ml/4fl oz/½ cup water in a small saucepan and stir over a low heat until the sugar has dissolved. Turn the heat up to medium and boil for 2 minutes until reduced and syrupy. Remove from the heat, add the ginger and mango slices and leave to cool.

5 Lift the rice out of the baking dish and remove the cling film. Using a wet knife, cut the rice into 16 pieces, each 4 x 2cm/1½ x ¾in. Arrange 1 piece of the mango on top of each rectangle of rice and arrange on a plate. Drizzle with the ginger syrup and serve.

VANILLA AND CINNAMON CUSTARD POTS WITH RHUBARB

SERVES 6

300ml/10½fl oz/scant 1¼ cups
   single cream
200ml/7fl oz/scant 1 cup milk
1 cinnamon stick
3 pieces star anise
1 tsp vanilla extract
3 eggs
5 tbsp caster sugar
soft dark brown sugar, to decorate

GINGER RHUBARB

400g/14oz rhubarb, cut into
   bite-sized pieces
6 tbsp caster sugar, or to taste
1–2 tsp ground ginger, to taste

1 Put the cream, milk, cinnamon stick and star anise in a saucepan and heat until almost boiling. Reduce the heat to low and simmer for 3 minutes, then turn off the heat, stir in the vanilla extract and leave to infuse for at least 30 minutes. Meanwhile, make the ginger rhubarb. Put the rhubarb, caster sugar, ginger and 3 tablespoons water in a non-reactive saucepan. Bring to the boil, then reduce the heat to low and simmer for 7 minutes until softened.

2 Using an electric whisk, whisk together the eggs and caster sugar until pale and creamy, then strain it into the cream mixture. Whisk again, then divide into six 185ml/6fl oz/¾ cup pots or ramekins.

3 Put the custards in a large steamer, cover and steam for 6–8 minutes until just set. Carefully remove from the steamer.

4 If serving warm, sprinkle the custard pots with brown sugar and serve with the rhubarb. Or leave the custard pots to cool, then chill for 2 hours. Just before serving, sprinkle with brown sugar and serve with the rhubarb.

CHOCOLATE PUDDINGS WITH MOCHA CREAM

SERVES 4

85g/3oz plain chocolate, around
   70% cocoa solids, grated, plus
   extra to decorate
170ml/5½fl oz/⅔ cup milk
55g/2oz butter, plus extra for
   greasing
55g/2oz/¼ cup caster sugar
3 eggs, separated
150g/5½oz/scant 2 cups fresh
   white breadcrumbs
1 tsp baking powder

MOCHA CREAM

2 tbsp milk
1 tbsp caster sugar
1 tbsp instant coffee granules
150ml/5fl oz/scant ⅔ cup double
   cream

1 Lightly grease four 250ml/9fl oz/1 cup pudding basins. Put the chocolate and milk in a heavy-based saucepan and warm over a low heat, stirring, until melted.

2 Using an electric mixer, cream the butter and sugar for 5 minutes until pale and fluffy. Beat in the egg yolks, then the chocolate mixture, breadcrumbs and baking powder. In a clean bowl, whisk the egg whites until they form stiff peaks, then fold them into the chocolate mixture. Divide the mixture into the pudding basins. Cover each with a circle of baking parchment, then with a circle of foil (both with a pleat down the centre). Secure with string.

3 Steam the puddings in a tiered steamer, or put them on an upturned plate in a large saucepan, adding enough water to come halfway up the sides of the basins. Cover and steam for 30 minutes, then set aside for 5 minutes to firm up before turning out.

4 Meanwhile, make the mocha cream. Warm the milk and sugar in a small saucepan over a medium-low heat, stirring, until the sugar has dissolved. Dissolve the coffee in 1 tablespoon boiling water and add it to the pan. Transfer to a mixing bowl and leave to cool. In a separate bowl, whisk the cream until soft peaks form, then stir it into the cooled coffee mixture. Serve the puddings with the mocha cream and a little extra chocolate grated over the tops.

SWEET HAZELNUT AND CHOCOLATE BUNS

These light, fluffy, Chinese-style buns can be made the day before and reheated in a steamer when ready to eat. They can also be frozen and then defrosted before steaming.

MAKES 16

1 ½ tsp dried active yeast
2 tbsp caster sugar
375g/13oz/3 cups plain flour, plus extra for kneading
1 tsp salt
1 tbsp sunflower oil, plus extra for greasing
1 ½ tsp baking powder

CHOCOLATE AND NUT FILLING
200g/7oz chocolate hazelnut spread
3 tbsp milk
4 tbsp chopped roasted almonds

1 To make the dough, stir together the yeast, caster sugar and 250ml/9fl oz/1 cup warm water in a small bowl until the sugar dissolves. Cover and leave to stand for 10 minutes until frothy.

2 Sift the flour and salt into a mixing bowl and make a well in the centre. Pour the yeast mixture and sunflower oil into the well and gradually mix in the flour to form a soft ball of dough – it should be quite sticky. Knead on a lightly floured surface for 10 minutes, adding a little more flour if necessary, until smooth and elastic.

3 Grease a clean mixing bowl with oil, add the dough and turn until coated. Cover with a clean damp tea towel and leave to rise in a warm place for 2½ hours, or until doubled in size.

4 Shape the dough into a round on a lightly floured surface and sprinkle with the baking powder. Knead for 5 minutes, then divide into 16 balls and cover with the damp tea towel.

5 Mix together the chocolate spread, milk and almonds for the filling. Press a ball of dough into a circle about 5mm/¼in thick and put 1 heaped tablespoonful of the chocolate mixture in the centre. Pull the edges up over the filling, press together to seal and set aside on a lightly floured surface. Repeat to make 16 buns.

6 Put 4–5 buns in a large bamboo steamer lined with baking parchment, spacing them slightly apart (or use a two-tiered steamer, if you have one). Cover and steam over a wok of simmering water for 15 minutes until risen and fluffy. If steaming in batches, cover the finished buns to keep warm while you cook the remaining ones. Replenish the steamer water as necessary to prevent it from boiling dry. Serve warm.

DATE AND ORANGE PUDDING WITH MARMALADE SAUCE

There is nothing quite like an old fashioned British steamed pudding – a perfect dessert for a cold winter's day. Towards the end of the cooking time, check the water levels in the pan to make sure it is not boiling dry.

SERVES 4

85g/3oz unsalted butter, plus extra for greasing

3 tbsp golden syrup

2 tbsp orange marmalade

juice of 2 oranges and finely grated zest of 1 orange

115g/4oz/²/₃ cup ready-to eat dried dates, coarsely chopped

85g/3oz/²/₃ cup self-raising flour

1 tsp bicarbonate of soda

a pinch of salt

90g/3¼ oz/½ cup soft light brown sugar

3 eggs

1 Lightly grease a 900ml/31fl oz/3¾ cups pudding basin with butter. In a small bowl, mix together the golden syrup and marmalade and spoon it into the base of the pudding basin.

2 Put the orange juice, zest and dates in a saucepan and bring to the boil, then reduce the heat to low and simmer for 10 minutes until the dates are very soft. Mash with a fork, then set aside to cool.

3 Sift together the flour, bicarbonate of soda and salt into a bowl. In another bowl, cream the butter and brown sugar with an electric mixer for 2 minutes until light and fluffy. Whisk in the eggs, one at a time, mixing well after each addition. Fold in the flour mixture, alternating with the mashed dates until well combined.

4 Pour the mixture into the basin and smooth the top. Cover with a round of baking parchment, then with a round of foil (both with a pleat down the centre) and secure with string. Put the basin on a trivet or upturned saucer in a large saucepan and add enough water to come halfway up the side of the basin. Cover with a tight-fitting lid and bring to a boil, then reduce the heat to medium-low and steam for 1 hour 15 minutes until risen. A skewer inserted in the centre of the pudding should come out clean.

5 Carefully remove the basin from the pan and leave to cool for a few minutes, then loosen with a knife, turn the pudding out on to a plate and serve.

Nurturing and nourishing, slow-simmered soups, stews and curries are as good for the soul as they are for the body. Gentle simmering techniques allow the flavours of individual ingredients to mingle, while more vigorous boiling transforms foods such as pasta, noodles and potatoes into the deliciously satisfying bases of many dishes.

SIMMER

Watermelon Curry on Black Lentil Cakes, page 171

SLOW-COOKED ONION AND CIDER SOUP WITH FONTINA CROÛTES

Slow cooking tempers the pungency of the onions, making them sweet and meltingly tender.

SERVES 4

4 tbsp olive oil
1kg/2lb 4oz onions, finely sliced
leaves from 10 thyme sprigs, plus
    extra to serve
2 bay leaves
3 large garlic cloves, chopped
185ml/6fl oz/¾ cup dry cider or dry
    white wine
900ml/31fl oz/3¾ cups vegetable
    stock
1 tbsp light soy sauce
salt and freshly ground black pepper

FONTINA CROÛTES

4 thick slices of ciabatta bread,
    sliced diagonally
150g/5½ oz Fontina cheese, rind
    removed and sliced

1 Heat the oil in a large saucepan over a medium-low to low heat and cook the onions, partially covered, for 35 minutes, stirring occasionally. Turn the heat to low if they start to brown too quickly. Remove the lid, then turn up the heat to medium and sauté, stirring occasionally, for another 5 minutes until the onions start to colour.

2 Add the thyme, bay leaves, garlic and cider and bring to the boil. Boil for 5 minutes or until the cider is reduced by half. Add the stock and return to the boil, then stir, reduce the heat to low and simmer, partially covered, for 30 minutes.

3 Add the soy sauce and season with salt and pepper. If preferred, the soup can be partially puréed: pour half of the soup into a blender and blend, then return to the pan and reheat, if necessary.

4 To make the Fontina croûtes, heat the grill to medium-high. Lightly toast one side of each slice of bread, then turn the slices over, top with the cheese and grill until melted and bubbling.

5 Ladle the soup into bowls and top with the croûtes. Sprinkle with a little extra thyme and serve immediately.

VEGETABLE, NORI AND NOODLE RAMEN

SERVES 4

2 eggs, at room temperature
175g/6oz ramen noodles
1 tbsp sunflower oil
2 leeks, thinly sliced
2 courgettes, thinly sliced
  diagonally
150g/5½ oz button mushrooms,
  sliced
3 handfuls of spinach leaves,
  shredded
175g/6oz Chinese leaves, sliced
1.5l/52fl oz/6 cups vegetable stock
3 tbsp light soy sauce
2 tbsp peeled, grated root ginger
1 tsp sesame oil
2 spring onions, finely chopped
¼ tsp dried chilli flakes
4 toasted nori strips, crumbled

1 Put the eggs in a saucepan of boiling water. Return to the boil, then reduce the heat to a simmer and cook for 6 minutes. Remove from the pan and rinse under cold running water for 1 minute. Set aside until cool enough to handle, then peel and cut in half lengthways.

2 Meanwhile, bring a large saucepan of water to the boil. Stir in the noodles to immerse them in the water and separate the strands. Return to the boil and cook over a medium-high heat for 4 minutes until tender. Drain and divide the noodles into four bowls.

3 While the noodles are cooking, heat the sunflower oil in a large saucepan over a medium-low heat and cook the leeks, courgettes and mushrooms for 2 minutes, then add the spinach and Chinese leaves and fry for 1 minute. Add the stock, soy sauce and ginger and bring to the boil, then reduce the heat to low and stir in the sesame oil. Heat through until the noodles have finished cooking.

4 Scoop out the vegetables from the soup with a slotted spoon and add to the bowls. Pour enough stock into each bowl to fill and sprinkle with spring onions, chilli flakes and nori. Top with half a hard-boiled egg and serve immediately.

COCONUT, LENTIL AND CHILLI SOUP

SERVES 4

2 tbsp sunflower oil
2 onions, finely chopped
2 tsp coriander seeds, crushed
1 chilli, split in half lengthways
2 garlic cloves, chopped
1 tbsp peeled and grated root ginger
1 lemongrass stick, finely chopped,
  with outer leaves removed
200g/7oz/scant 1 cup dried red
  lentils, rinsed
900ml/31fl oz/3¾ cups vegetable
  stock
1 tbsp tomato purée
400ml/14fl oz/1⅔ cups coconut
  milk
juice of 1 lime
4 tbsp coriander leaves, chopped
2 spring onions, finely chopped
salt and freshly ground black pepper

1 Heat the oil in a large saucepan over a medium-low heat and fry the onions for 8 minutes until softened. Add the coriander seeds, chilli, garlic, ginger and lemongrass and cook for another 1 minute.

2 Add the lentils and stir to coat them in the oil and spices, then add the stock and bring to the boil. Reduce the heat to low and simmer, partially covered, for 20 minutes. Stir in the tomato purée and coconut milk and continue to simmer for 15–20 minutes until the lentils are soft and breaking down into the soup.

3 Add the lime juice and 3 tablespoons of the coriander leaves and season to taste with salt and pepper. Ladle the soup into four bowls, sprinkle with the remaining coriander leaves and spring onions, then serve immediately.

JERUSALEM ARTICHOKE SOUP

Quirky, oddly shaped Jerusalem artichokes make a remarkably good thick soup, thanks to their mildly nutty flavour. The truffle oil is an optional decadence.

SERVES 4

2 tbsp olive oil

1 large onion, chopped

1 celery stick, chopped

1 carrot, sliced

1 large garlic clove, chopped

680g/1lb 8oz Jerusalem artichokes, scrubbed or peeled, and chopped

1.25l/44fl oz/5 cups vegetable stock

250ml/9fl oz/1 cup milk

4 thick slices of sourdough bread, crusts removed

truffle oil, for drizzling (optional)

55g/2oz grated Parmesan cheese

salt and freshly ground black pepper

1 Heat the oil in a large saucepan over a medium-low heat and sauté the onion for 6 minutes or until softened. Add the celery, carrot, garlic and Jerusalem artichokes and sauté for another 5 minutes, stirring occasionally.

2 Add the stock and bring to the boil, then reduce the heat to low and simmer for 25 minutes, stirring occasionally, until the vegetables are tender. Using a hand-held blender, purée the soup until smooth. Stir in the milk, season with salt and pepper and warm through.

3 Meanwhile, toast the slices of bread and cut into cubes. Spoon the soup into four bowls, then top with the croûtons and drizzle with a little truffle oil, if using. Sprinkle a heap of the Parmesan into the centre and serve.

SPICED APPLE AND PARSNIP SOUP WITH PARSNIP CRISPS

SERVES 4

500g/1lb 2oz parsnips, peeled

6 tbsp sunflower oil

1 large onion, chopped

1 celery stick, thinly sliced

1 bay leaf

1 tsp ground cumin

1 tsp ground coriander

½ tsp turmeric

½–1 tsp dried chilli flakes

900ml/31fl oz/3¾ cups vegetable stock

2 slightly sharp apples, peeled, cored and diced

2 tsp lemon juice

salt and freshly ground black pepper

1 Slice 4 of the parsnips and use a vegetable peeler to cut the remaining parsnip lengthways into thin ribbons.

2 Heat 1 tablespoon of the sunflower oil in a large saucepan and cook the onion, partially covered, for 6 minutes, stirring occasionally, until softened. Add the celery, sliced parsnips, bay leaf, cumin, coriander, turmeric and chilli flakes and cook for 2 minutes, stirring regularly. Add the stock, bring to the boil, then reduce the heat to medium-low. Cook, partially covered, for 10 minutes, stirring occasionally.

3 Add the apples and cook for 6–8 minutes until softened, then stir in the lemon juice. Using a hand-held blender, purée the soup until smooth. Taste and add more chilli if desired, then season with salt and pepper.

4 Heat the remaining oil in a frying pan and fry the parsnip ribbons for 2–3 minutes or until crisp and golden. Drain on kitchen paper.

5 Reheat the soup and ladle it into four bowls. Top with the crisp parsnip ribbons and serve.

WAKAME, RADISH AND NOODLE SALAD

SERVES 4

20g/¾ oz dried wakame, cut into
 small pieces or strips

2 tbsp pumpkin seeds, toasted

100g/3½ oz vermicelli rice noodles

200g/7oz radishes, cut into thin
 rounds

1 small cucumber, deseeded and cut
 into ribbons

80g/2¾ oz mooli, peeled and cut
 into matchsticks

2 tbsp pink pickled ginger

2 tbsp shiso sprouts or radish
 sprouts

SESAME—MIRIN DRESSING

2 tbsp sunflower or rapeseed oil

1 tbsp sesame oil

2 tbsp light soy sauce

3 tbsp rice wine vinegar

2 tbsp mirin

1 tbsp peeled and finely grated root
 ginger

salt and freshly ground black pepper

1 Soak the wakame in a bowl of warm water for 10—15 minutes until rehydrated. Drain, rinse under cold running water and drain again.

2 Meanwhile, toast the pumpkin seeds in a dry frying pan over a medium-low heat for 3—4 minutes, stirring occasionally. Watch carefully as they easily burn.

3 Put the noodles in a heatproof bowl and soak in just-boiled water for 3—5 minutes until softened. Rinse, then refresh under cold running water. Put the noodles, wakame, radishes, cucumber and mooli in a bowl.

4 Mix together all of the ingredients for the dressing and pour it over the salad. Toss lightly until combined.

5 Divide the salad into four bowls and sprinkle with the pumpkin seeds. Arrange the pickled ginger and shiso sprouts in a heap on top and serve.

SHAOXING TOFU WITH STAR ANISE

SERVES 4

1 tbsp sesame oil

2.5cm/1in piece of root ginger,
 peeled and cut into matchsticks

125ml/4fl oz/½ cup Shaoxing wine

2 star anise

4 tbsp hoisin sauce

2 tbsp dark soy sauce

400g/14oz firm tofu, patted dry and
 cut into 1cm/½ in-thick slices

2 spring onions, thinly sliced
 diagonally

1 Heat a large wok over a medium-high heat. Add the sesame oil and the ginger and fry, stirring occasionally, for 1 minute. Add the Shaoxing wine and cook for 2—3 minutes until reduced by half, then stir in the star anise, hoisin sauce, soy sauce and tofu.

2 Reduce the heat to low and simmer for 5 minutes, occasionally spooning the sauce over the tofu. Using a spatula, remove the tofu from the wok and set aside. Increase the heat to medium-low and cook the sauce for 2—3 minutes until reduced and thickened.

3 Divide the tofu into four shallow bowls and spoon the sauce over it. Sprinkle with the spring onions and serve.

MUSTARD AND LEMON PUY LENTILS WITH ZA'ATAR EGGS

Za'atar is a Middle Eastern condiment made from herbs, sesame seeds, salt and sumac and sometimes other spices. It is often mixed with olive oil and used as a spread on bread, a seasoning or, as here, a coating.

SERVES 4

250g/9oz/ 1 ¼ cups Puy lentils

2 bay leaves

4 eggs, at room temperature

2 tbsp olive oil

1 large onion, chopped

1 celery stick, finely sliced

1 large red pepper, deseeded and diced

3 large garlic cloves, chopped

6 plum tomatoes, deseeded and diced

100ml/3 ½ fl oz/scant ½ cup hot vegetable stock

juice of 1 lemon

finely grated zest of ½ lemon

1 tbsp Dijon mustard

4 heaped tbsp crème fraîche

4 tbsp chopped flat-leaf parsley leaves

freshly ground black pepper

ZA'ATAR SPICE MIX

1 tbsp sesame seeds

1 tbsp ground sumac

2 tbsp thyme leaves

1 tsp salt, crushed, plus extra to taste

1 Put the lentils and bay leaves in a saucepan, cover with water and bring to the boil. Reduce the heat to low and simmer, partially covered, for 25 minutes or until the lentils are tender, then drain.

2 Meanwhile, put the eggs in a small saucepan of boiling water. Return to the boil, then reduce the heat to a simmer and cook the eggs for 6 minutes. Remove the eggs from the pan and rinse under cold running water for 1 minute to prevent them cooking further, then set aside.

3 Heat the olive oil in a large frying pan and fry the onion for 10 minutes, stirring occasionally, until softened and golden. Add the celery and red pepper and fry for 3 minutes, then add the garlic and cook for 1 minute, stirring occasionally. Stir in the tomatoes, stock, lemon juice, lemon zest, mustard, crème fraîche and lentils. Cook 2–3 minutes until warmed through and the tomatoes start to soften.

4 Meanwhile, to make the za'atar spice mix, toast the sesame seeds in a dry frying pan over a medium heat for 2–3 minutes, stirring occasionally, until lightly browned. Remove from the heat and mix with the remaining za'atar ingredients in a small bowl. Peel the eggs and roll them in the za'atar. (Store any leftover za'atar in an airtight jar for up to three weeks.)

5 Season the lentils with salt and pepper and stir in the parsley, then spoon them into four large, shallow bowls. Cut the eggs in half lengthways, put 2 halves on top of each portion of lentils and serve.

SPRING VEGETABLE AND LEMON TAGLIATELLE

SERVES 4

375g/13oz dried egg tagliatelle
275g/9¾ oz asparagus tips
2 courgettes, sliced into long vertical
    strips, then halved lengthways
4 spring onions, sliced diagonally
juice of 1 small lemon
200g/7oz rindless goat's cheese,
    crumbled
salt and freshly ground black pepper
basil leaves, to serve

GARLIC CRUMBS

5 tbsp olive oil
115g/4oz/2 cups fresh
    breadcrumbs
2 large garlic cloves, finely chopped
grated zest of 1 small lemon
1 red chilli, deseeded and sliced

1 First make the garlic crumbs. Heat 2 tablespoons of the olive oil
   in a frying pan over a medium heat and fry the breadcrumbs for
   2 minutes, stirring occasionally, until beginning to crisp. Add the
   garlic, lemon zest and chilli and cook for another 2–3 minutes until
   the crumbs are golden, then set aside.

2 Cook the tagliatelle according to the packet instructions until al
   dente, then drain, reserving 125ml/4fl oz/½ cup of the cooking
   water. Meanwhile, steam the asparagus and courgettes for 3–5
   minutes until just tender, then refresh under cold running water.

3 Heat the rest of the olive oil in a large frying pan over a medium-low
   heat and fry the spring onions for 1 minute, stirring occasionally.
   Add the cooked pasta and reserved cooking water and turn until
   coated. Add the courgettes, asparagus, lemon juice and half of
   the garlic crumbs and warm through, tossing well. Season with
   salt and pepper.

4 Divide the tagliatelle on to four plates and top with the goat's
   cheese and remaining garlic crumbs. Sprinkle with basil and serve.

RED QUINOA AND SPINACH SALAD WITH PECANS AND HALLOUMI

SERVES 4

150g/5½ oz/¾ cup red quinoa
250g/9oz halloumi cheese, sliced
olive oil, for brushing
2 tbsp ras-el-hanout
55g/2oz/½ cup pecan halves
4 tbsp pumpkin seeds
2 large handfuls of baby leaf spinach
6 unsulphured dried apricots,
    chopped
1 small red onion, thinly sliced
4 tbsp chopped flat-leaf parsley

POMEGRANATE DRESSING

3 tbsp pomegranate molasses
1 tbsp lemon juice
3 tbsp olive oil
1 garlic clove, crushed
½ tsp caster sugar
a pinch of ground cumin
salt and freshly ground black pepper

1 Put the quinoa in a saucepan and cover with water. Bring to the boil,
   reduce the heat to low and simmer, covered, for 10–15 minutes
   until tender. Drain well and set aside to cool in a bowl.

2 Brush the halloumi with olive oil and dust it in the ras-el-hanout.
   Heat a griddle pan over a high heat until it almost starts to smoke.
   Reduce the heat to medium and grill the halloumi for 3–4 minutes,
   turning once, until the griddle marks are visible but the cheese still
   remains a little soft.

3 Meanwhile, toast the pecans in a single layer in a dry frying pan
   over a medium-low heat for 2–3 minutes, turning halfway through.
   Remove from the pan and repeat with the pumpkin seeds.

4 In a small bowl, mix together all of the ingredients for the dressing
   and add it to the quinoa. Add the spinach, apricots, red onion, and
   parsley and toss until coated. Divide on to four plates and top with
   the pecans, pumpkin seeds and halloumi and serve.

BHEL PURI ON POPPADOM CRISPS

This delicious Indian-inspired salad is a perfect example of how you can transform simple ingredients into something very special. Some brands of tamarind paste contain the seeds; if so, pick them out before use.

SERVES 4

450g/1lb new potatoes, halved

200g/7oz/1½ cups cooked chickpeas

2 red chillies, deseeded and chopped

1 small red onion, finely chopped

4 heaped tbsp chopped coriander leaves

4 uncooked poppadoms

sunflower oil, for frying

4 tomatoes, deseeded and diced

salt and freshly ground black pepper

TAMARIND AND YOGURT DRESSING

3 tbsp tamarind paste

2.5cm/1in piece of root ginger, peeled and finely chopped

½ tsp ground cumin

1 tbsp lemon juice

5 tbsp natural yogurt

1 Cook the potatoes in boiling salted water for 10 minutes or until tender. Drain and set aside until cool enough to handle, then peel off the skins. Dice the potatoes and transfer to a bowl. Add the chickpeas, chillies, red onion and 3 tablespoons of the coriander leaves. Season with salt and pepper.

2 Put all of the ingredients for the dressing and 1 tablespoon water in a food processor and process until almost smooth. Pour the dressing over the potato salad and mix gently until well combined. Set aside.

3 To cook the poppadoms, heat 5cm/2in of the sunflower oil in a wide saucepan over a medium-high heat until it reaches 190°C/375°F – a cube of bread will turn golden in 20 seconds when dropped into the oil. Cook the poppadoms, one at a time, holding them under the oil with a spatula for 2–3 seconds until puffed up and crisp. Drain on kitchen paper.

4 To serve, put each poppadom on a plate and pile one-quarter of the potato salad on top of each one. Top with the tomatoes and remaining coriander leaves and serve at room temperature.

WINTER VEGETABLE AND COFFEE STEW WITH CHEESE DUMPLINGS

The intensity of the coffee in this recipe lends a depth and richness to the stock, without being overpowering in flavour.

SERVES 4

2 tbsp olive oil

2 onions, chopped

1 celery stick, sliced

1 leek, sliced

2 turnips, peeled and cut into bite-sized pieces

2 parsnips, peeled and cut into bite-sized pieces

250g/9oz baby carrots, trimmed

75g/2½oz shiitake mushrooms, sliced

1 tbsp plain flour

6 thyme sprigs

1 bay leaf

200ml/7fl oz/scant 1 cup strong brewed coffee

250ml/9fl oz/1 cup vegetable stock

2 tbsp dark soy sauce

400g/14oz/1½ cups cooked borlotti beans

salt and freshly ground black pepper

CHEESE DUMPLINGS

90g/3¼oz/¾ cup self-raising flour

40g/1½oz/⅓ cup grated mature Cheddar cheese

2 tbsp chopped parsley leaves

40g/1½oz softened butter, cut into small pieces

1 Heat the oil in a large flameproof casserole dish over a medium-low heat and fry the onions for 6 minutes, stirring occasionally, until softened. Add the celery and leek and sauté for another 2 minutes, then add the turnips, parsnips, carrots and shiitake mushrooms. Stir in the flour and cook for 1 minute, stirring, then add the thyme and bay leaf. Add the coffee, stock, soy sauce and borlotti beans and bring to the boil, then reduce the heat to low and simmer for 10 minutes, stirring occasionally. Season with salt and pepper.

2 Meanwhile, make the dumplings. Mix together the flour, Cheddar, parsley and butter in a bowl. Stir in 1 tablespoon water and bring the mixture together with your hands to make a firm ball of dough. Divide the dough into 8 equal-sized pieces and shape them into balls.

3 Arrange the dumplings in the casserole so they are half submerged in the vegetable mixture. Cover with a lid and simmer over a low heat for 20–25 minutes until the dumplings have risen and the vegetables are tender. Serve hot.

MUSHROOM AND CHESTNUT RAGOÛT WITH SWEET POTATO MASH

Simmered over a low heat, the mushrooms really absorb the flavours of the sherry and soy to produce a dark, potent stew with a rich, earthy taste.

SERVES 4

40g/1½oz dried porcini mushrooms

3 tbsp olive oil

40g/1½oz butter

350g/12oz shallots, peeled and halved with the base intact, or quartered if large

500g/1lb 2oz portobello mushrooms, thickly sliced

2 tsp dried thyme

125ml/4fl oz/½ cup dry sherry

250g/9oz cooked chestnuts, thickly sliced

2 tbsp light soy sauce

a few splashes of hot-pepper sauce

5 tbsp double cream

leaves from a few parsley sprigs, chopped

salt and freshly ground black pepper

SWEET POTATO MASH

900g/2lb sweet potatoes, peeled and cut into chunks

2 large garlic cloves

150ml/5fl oz/scant ⅔ cup milk

30g/1oz butter

1 Soak the porcini mushrooms in 150ml/5fl oz/scant ⅔ cup boiled water for 20 minutes until softened.

2 Heat the olive oil and butter in a large, heavy-based saucepan over a medium-low heat and cook the shallots for 12 minutes, stirring regularly, until softened and golden in places. Add the portobello mushrooms and cook for another 4–5 minutes until tender.

3 Strain the porcini mushrooms, reserving the soaking liquid, and add them to the pan, along with the thyme and sherry. Bring to the boil, then reduce the heat to low and simmer until the liquid has reduced by half and there is no aroma of alcohol.

4 Add the porcini soaking liquid, chestnuts, soy sauce and hot-pepper sauce and simmer for 10–15 minutes until reduced by half. Stir in the cream and heat through gently, then season with salt and pepper.

5 Meanwhile, make the sweet potato mash. Cook the sweet potatoes and garlic in boiling salted water for 10 minutes or until tender, then drain and return to the pan. Add the milk and butter, season well with salt and pepper and warm through. Mash until smooth, then cover with a lid to keep warm.

6 Sprinkle the ragoût with the parsley and serve with the sweet potato mash.

SPLIT PEA AND PANEER CURRY

Split peas benefit from long, slow cooking to give them time to break down and thicken the sauce. This curry can be made up to three days in advance and reheated, which allows the flavours to meld and intensify.

SERVES 4

200g/7oz/heaped ¾ cup yellow split peas, rinsed
3 tbsp sunflower oil
2 onions, finely chopped
3 garlic cloves, chopped
5cm/2in piece of root ginger, peeled and grated
2 tsp yellow mustard seeds
2 tsp cumin seeds
1 tsp fennel seeds
1 large red chilli, deseeded and chopped
1 tsp turmeric
1 tsp ground coriander
2 carrots, diced
3 curry leaf sprigs
200ml/7fl oz/scant 1 cup passata
300ml/10½fl oz/scant 1¼ cups vegetable stock
300ml/10½fl oz/scant 1¼ cups coconut milk
225g/8oz paneer cheese, cubed
salt and freshly ground black pepper
coriander leaves, to serve

1 Put the yellow split peas in a large saucepan and cover with plenty of water. Bring to the boil, then reduce the heat to low and simmer, partially covered, for 40 minutes or until tender. Occasionally skim off any foam that rises to the surface. Drain and return to the pan.

2 Heat the sunflower oil in a large frying pan over a medium-low heat and fry the onions for 10 minutes until softened and turning golden. Stir in the garlic, ginger and mustard, cumin and fennel seeds and cook for 2 minutes, then stir in the chilli, turmeric and ground coriander. Add the mixture to the pan with the split peas.

3 Add the carrots, curry leaves, passata and stock. Bring to the boil, then reduce the heat to low and simmer, partially covered, for 10 minutes. Stir in the coconut milk and paneer and simmer, stirring occasionally, for another 10 minutes until thickened. Season with salt and pepper, then sprinkle with coriander leaves and serve.

GNOCCHI WITH SQUASH AND TOASTED WALNUTS IN SAGE BUTTER

There are many versions of gnocchi, depending on where you are in Italy. The ratio of potato to flour as well as the inclusion of eggs vary greatly as does the shape and size of these little pasta dumplings, literally translated as 'little lumps'.

SERVES 4

550g/1lb 4oz even-sized floury-type
   potatoes, unpeeled
200g/7oz/heaped 1½ cups Italian
   00 plain flour or regular plain flour,
   plus extra for rolling
1 egg, lightly beaten
salt and freshly ground black pepper
freshly grated Parmesan or pecorino
   cheese, to serve

SAUCE

550g/1lb 4oz butternut squash
   or other type of squash, peeled,
   deseeded and cut into bite-sized
   chunks
6 tbsp olive oil
125g/4½oz/1¼ cups walnut
   halves
70g/2½oz butter
1 small handful of sage leaves,
   coarsely chopped

1 Cook the potatoes in boiling water for 20 minutes until tender. Drain and when cool enough to handle, peel off the skins. Sift the flour into a bowl, make a well in the centre and add the egg. Grate the potatoes (or press them through a sieve or mouli) on to the flour and egg. Season with salt and mix thoroughly, kneading to make a soft dough – you may need to add a little extra flour.

2 With floured hands, roll the dough into a sausage shape, about 1.5cm/⅝in in diameter and then cut into 2cm/¾in pieces. Press a finger into each piece to flatten slightly, then draw your finger towards you to curl the sides. Chill the gnocchi until ready to cook.

3 Meanwhile, roast the squash for the sauce. Preheat the oven to 200°C/400°F/gas 6 and grease a baking tray with 1 tablespoon of the olive oil. Roast the squash for 20 minutes until tender, turning halfway. Put the walnuts on a clean baking sheet and bake for 3–5 minutes until toasted. Leave to cool slightly, then chop coarsely.

4 Bring a large saucepan of salted water to the boil and cook the gnocchi, about 20 at a time, for 2–3 minutes or until they float to the top. Remove from the water using a slotted spoon and transfer to a plate. Cover to keep warm while you cook the remaining gnocchi.

5 Heat the remaining oil and butter in a large saucepan over a medium-low heat. Fry the sage for 1 minute, stirring, then add the squash and half of the walnuts. Stir in the cooked gnocchi and gently turn until coated, adding a splash of water if too dry. Sprinkle with the reserved walnuts and Parmesan and serve.

AUBERGINE, APRICOT AND ALMOND TAGINE

'Tagine' refers both to the earthenware cooking pot with a shallow base and conical lid and the Moroccan stew that is cooked in it. There are numerous versions of a tagine but the essence of the dish is that it is simmered slowly and gently to create an intensely flavoured aromatic sauce. The addition of dried apricots here lends a rich sweetness to the stew, while the spice mix ras-el-hanout ensures an authentic flavour.

SERVES 4

2 tbsp olive oil

30g/1oz butter

1 large onion, sliced

1 large aubergine, cut into 2.5cm/ 1in dice

2 large garlic cloves, chopped

2 courgettes, thickly sliced

2 tbsp ras-el-hanout

½ tsp dried chilli flakes

225g/8oz sweet potatoes, peeled and cut into 2.5cm/1in dice

600ml/21fl oz/scant 2½ cups passata

1 tbsp tomato purée

1 tbsp clear honey

80g/2¾ oz dried apricots

400g/14oz/1½ cups cooked chickpeas

55g/2oz/⅓ cup whole blanched almonds

salt and freshly ground black pepper

1 small handful of coriander leaves, chopped, to serve

cooked couscous, to serve

1 Heat the olive oil and butter in a tagine or large, wide saucepan over a medium heat. Add the onion and sauté over a medium-low heat for 6 minutes, stirring regularly. Add the aubergine, garlic and courgettes and cook for another 5 minutes, stirring occasionally, until the vegetables have softened.

2 Add the ras-el-hanout and stir until the vegetables are coated in the spices. Add the dried chilli flakes, sweet potatoes, passata, tomato purée, honey and 150ml/5fl oz/scant ⅔ cup water and bring to the boil, then stir until combined and reduce the heat to low.

3 Simmer, covered, for 15 minutes, stirring occasionally, until the sauce begins to thicken. Stir in the apricot and chickpeas, cover again and cook for another 15 minutes until the vegetables are tender. Add a little extra water if the tagine becomes too dry. Season with salt and pepper

4 Meanwhile, preheat the oven to 180°C/350°F/gas 4. Put the almonds on a baking sheet and bake for 5–6 minutes until toasted. Remove from the oven and set aside to cool.

5 Sprinkle the tagine with the coriander leaves and toasted almonds and serve with couscous.

MINTED PEA AND LEEK RISOTTO WITH SOFT POACHED EGG

The secret to a good risotto is firstly the right rice: use arborio, carnaroli or vialone as they give a wonderful creamy, velvety texture when cooked, yet the grain retains a little 'bite' in the centre. Equally important is adding the hot stock gradually and gently stirring until it is absorbed.

SERVES 4

2 tbsp olive oil

2 leeks, finely chopped

350g/12oz/scant 1²/₃ cups arborio rice

170ml/5½ fl oz/²/₃ cup dry white wine

300g/10½ oz frozen petit pois

1 handful of mint leaves, chopped

1 handful of basil leaves, plus extra to serve

1.5l/52fl oz/6 cups hot vegetable stock

100g/3½ oz/1 cup Parmesan cheese, finely grated, plus extra to serve

4 eggs

salt and freshly ground black pepper

1 Heat the olive oil in a large, heavy-based saucepan over a medium heat. Add the leeks, cover and reduce the heat to medium-low. Cook for 5 minutes, stirring occasionally, until softened. Add the rice and stir for 2 minutes to coat it in the oil. Add the wine and bring to the boil over a medium-high heat, then reduce the heat to medium-low and cook until absorbed by the rice.

2 Meanwhile, steam the peas for 3 minutes until tender, then transfer to a blender. Add the mint, basil and 100ml/3½ fl oz/scant ½ cup of the stock and blend until puréed, then set aside.

3 Add a ladleful of hot stock to the rice and cook, stirring continuously with a wooden spoon, until the rice has absorbed the liquid. Continue to add the stock, a ladleful at a time, stirring to allow the rice to cook evenly and to prevent it from sticking to the bottom of the pan, until all the stock has been used and the rice is cooked and creamy but still retains a slight bite. This will take about 25 minutes. Remove the pan from the heat and stir in the pea purée and Parmesan.

4 Bring a large sauté pan of water to the boil, then reduce the heat to low. Break 1 egg into a cup and then slip it out of the cup into the gently simmering water. Repeat with the 3 remaining eggs and simmer for 3–4 minutes, occasionally spooning the water over the top of each one, until the white is set but the yolk remains soft.

5 While the eggs are cooking, warm through the risotto, then season with salt and pepper. Divide the risotto into four shallow bowls and top with a poached egg. Sprinkle with extra Parmesan and basil leaves and serve immediately.

WATERMELON CURRY ON BLACK LENTIL CAKES

Watermelon makes a wonderfully vibrant, fresh tasting curry. Toast the whole spices first in a dry frying pan to enrich the flavour of the sauce.

SERVES 4

4cm/1 ½ in piece of root ginger, peeled
2 large garlic cloves, chopped
1 tbsp sunflower oil
2 tsp cumin seeds
1 tsp fenugreek seeds
1 long red chilli, deseeded and finely chopped
2.25kg/5lb watermelon, skin removed, deseeded and cut into bite-sized chunks
2 tsp turmeric
2 tsp ground coriander
2 tbsp lime juice
2 tbsp shredded mint leaves
salt and freshly ground black pepper

BLACK LENTIL CAKES

225g/8oz/1 ¼ cups whole black lentils
1 tbsp sunflower oil, plus extra for frying
1 large onion, finely chopped
2 large garlic cloves, chopped
2 tsp cumin seeds
2 tsp garam masala
2 tsp ground coriander
1 tsp hot chilli powder
1 egg, lightly beaten
3 tbsp plain flour, plus extra for coating

1 First make the black lentil cakes. Put the lentils in a saucepan, cover with water and bring to the boil. Reduce the heat to low and simmer, partially covered, for 40 minutes or until the lentils are very tender. Drain, then transfer to a mixing bowl and roughly mash with a potato masher or the back of a fork. Set aside to cool.

2 Meanwhile, heat the sunflower oil for the lentil cakes in a frying pan over a medium-low heat and fry the onion for 8 minutes, stirring occasionally, until softened. Add the garlic and cumin and cook for 1 minute. Stir in the garam masala, coriander and chilli powder and then add the mixture to the bowl with the lentils. Stir in the egg and flour and season well with salt and pepper.

3 With floured hands, divide the lentil mixture into 4 equal portions and shape each one into a cake, then lightly coat each one in a little flour. The mixture is quite loose, so press the burger firmly until it holds its shape – the flour will help to achieve this. Put the burgers on a plate and chill until ready to cook.

4 To make the watermelon curry, purée the ginger and garlic in a food processor until they form a paste. Heat the sunflower oil in a frying pan over a medium heat and fry the paste for 1 minute, stirring occasionally. Stir in the cumin and fenugreek seeds and cook for another 1 minute, then add the red chilli.

5 Purée half of the watermelon in the food processor and add it to the frying pan along with the turmeric and ground coriander. Bring to the boil, then reduce the heat to low and simmer for 10 minutes or until reduced by half and thickened.

6 Meanwhile, cook the lentil cakes. Heat enough oil to generously coat a large, non-stick frying pan over a medium heat. Add the cakes, flattening slightly with a spatula, and fry for 2–3 minutes on each side until crisp.

7 Add the lime juice and remaining watermelon to the curry and season with salt and pepper. Cook for another 5–8 minutes until softened.

8 Put 1 lentil cake on each of four plates and top with the watermelon curry. Sprinkle with the mint and serve.

BLACK BEAN MOLE WITH CHICKPEA PANCAKES

There are many versions of the classic Mexican mole sauce, spiked with chilli, spices and a hint of dark chocolate. While the chipotle chilli is not strictly authentic, it lends a delicious smokiness and hint of tobacco. The mole is served with chickpea pancakes, with their distinctive golden colour and flavour.

SERVES 4

400g/14oz acorn squash, peeled, deseeded and cut into bite-sized chunks

40g/1½oz/¼ cup blanched almonds

2 tbsp olive oil

1 large onion, chopped

3 garlic cloves, chopped

1 dried chipotle chilli, finely chopped or 3 tbsp chipotle paste

1 dried ancho chilli, finely chopped

½–1 tsp dried chilli flakes

2 tsp paprika

½ tsp cinnamon

1 tsp ground cumin

½ tsp ground allspice

600ml/21fl oz/scant 2½ cups passata

2 bay leaves

2 tsp dark brown sugar

40g/1½oz dark chocolate, chopped

275g/9¾oz/scant 2 cups cooked black beans

finely grated zest of ½ lime, plus extra to serve

6 tbsp crème fraîche

salt and freshly ground black pepper

1 avocado, to serve

CHICKPEA PANCAKES

225g/8oz/heaped 1¾ cups chickpea flour

1 tsp bicarbonate of soda

1 tsp salt

sunflower oil, for frying

1 To make the chickpea pancakes, sift the chickpea flour, bicarbonate of soda and salt into a large mixing bowl. Make a well in the centre and pour in 400ml/14fl oz/scant 1⅔ cups water. Gradually whisk the flour into the water to make a smooth batter. Leave to stand for 20 minutes or until ready to cook.

2 Steam the squash for 6 minutes or until tender, then set aside. Meanwhile, toast the almonds in a dry frying pan over a medium-low heat, stirring occasionally, for 3–4 minutes, then set aside to cool.

3 Heat the olive oil in a large pan over a medium-low heat and fry the onion for 8 minutes until softened. Add the garlic, chipotle, ancho, chilli flakes, paprika, cinnamon, cumin and allspice and cook for 2 minutes, stirring. Add the passata, bay leaves and 125ml/4fl oz/½ cup water and bring to the boil, then reduce the heat to low and simmer, partially covered, for 10 minutes.

4 Grind the almonds in a food processor until fine, then add them to the sauce. Add the brown sugar and chocolate and stir until the chocolate has melted. Add the black beans and simmer, covered, for 20 minutes, stirring regularly to prevent the sauce from sticking. Stir in the squash, season with salt and pepper and warm through.

5 Meanwhile, cook the pancakes. Preheat the oven to 70°C/150°F/gas ¼. Add enough sunflower oil to lightly coat the base of a non-stick frying pan and heat over a medium heat. For each pancake, put 4 tablespoons of the batter in the pan and cook for 2–3 minutes on each side until golden. Work in batches, if necessary, keeping the finished pancakes warm in the oven and adding more oil to the pan as necessary.

6 Stir the lime zest into the crème fraîche, then peel, stone and slice the avocado. Top the mole with the crème fraîche and avocado and serve accompanied by the chickpea pancakes and sprinkled with extra lime zest.

CREAMY CHARD, PORCINI AND PARMESAN PAPPARDELLE

SERVES 4–6

30g/1oz dried porcini mushrooms

375g/13oz dried egg pappardelle

3 tbsp olive oil

200g/7oz portobellini mushrooms, sliced

200ml/7fl oz/scant 1 cup dry white wine

200g/7oz rainbow chard, stalks thinly sliced and leaves thickly sliced

200g/7oz/1 cup crème fraîche

70g/2½oz/¾ cup Parmesan cheese, finely grated

salt and freshly ground black pepper

1 Soak the porcini mushrooms in 250ml/9fl oz/1 cup boiling water for 20 minutes until softened. Drain, reserving the soaking liquid, and coarsely chop.

2 Cook the pappardelle in plenty of boiling salted water according to the packet instructions and drain.

3 Meanwhile, heat the olive oil in a large sauté pan over a medium heat and fry the porcini for 4 minutes until almost crisp, then add the portobellini mushrooms and fry for another 4 minutes until softened. Add the wine and bring to the boil, then cook over a medium-high heat for 5 minutes until it has reduced by half. Add the reserved soaking liquid and cook for 3 minutes or until reduced.

4 Meanwhile, steam the chard for 2–3 minutes until softened.

5 Stir the crème fraîche into the mushroom mixture, season well with salt and pepper and then stir in half of the Parmesan. Add the drained pasta and chard and turn until coated. Sprinkle with the remaining Parmesan, season with salt and pepper and serve.

CHEESY POLENTA MASH WITH SHALLOT AND FENNEL CONFIT

SERVES 4

100ml/3½fl oz/scant ½ cup olive oil

400g/14oz shallots, peeled and quartered with the base intact or cut into 6 wedges, if large

1 aubergine, cut into bite-sized pieces

1 large fennel bulb, cut into 8 wedges

3 tbsp apple juice

1 tbsp balsamic vinegar

1 tsp soft brown sugar

salt and freshly ground black pepper

CHEESY POLENTA MASH

175g/6oz/scant 1¼ cups instant polenta

40g/1½oz butter

55g/2oz/½ cup Parmesan cheese, finely grated

1 Heat the olive oil over a medium heat in a deep sauté pan. Add the shallots in a single layer and sauté for 7 minutes, stirring occasionally. Stir in the aubergine and fennel, then cover with a lid and cook over a low heat for 25 minutes, stirring occasionally to prevent the vegetables from sticking to the base of the pan.

2 Add the apple juice, balsamic vinegar and brown sugar, then season with salt and pepper. Stir well and cook for another 10 minutes until the vegetables are very tender and the balsamic vinegar has reduced.

3 Meanwhile, make the polenta. Heat 850ml/29fl oz/scant 3½ cups water in a saucepan, sprinkle in the polenta and bring to the boil, stirring frequently. Reduce the heat to low and simmer, stirring frequently, for 5–6 minutes until smooth and creamy (it should be the same consistency as mashed potato). Stir in the butter and Parmesan and season with salt and pepper. Serve with the confit.

ORIENTAL BLACK BEAN AND SHIITAKE RISOTTO

Chinese rice wine, fermented black beans and shiitake mushrooms, with their rich, almost meaty, flavour, add an oriental twist to this classic creamy risotto. If desired, the risotto can be half cooked ahead of time, then, just before serving, reheat the stock and continue as instructed in step 4.

SERVES 4

3 tbsp Chinese fermented black
   beans
2 tbsp olive oil
2 onions, diced
5cm/2in piece of root ginger, peeled
   and cut into matchsticks
200g/7oz chestnut mushrooms,
   halved
200g/7oz shiitake mushrooms,
   sliced
350g/12oz/scant 1²/₃ cups arborio
   rice
170ml/5½fl oz/²/₃ cup Chinese
   cooking wine or dry sherry
1.5l/52fl oz/6 cups hot vegetable
   stock
2 tbsp light soy sauce
4 tbsp chopped coriander leaves
2 tbsp finely chopped chives
freshly ground black pepper

1 Soak the black beans in 3 tablespoons hot water for 20 minutes, then drain and set aside.

2 Heat the olive oil in a large, heavy-based saucepan over a medium-low heat. Add the onions and cook, covered, for 8 minutes, stirring occasionally, until softened. Add the black beans, ginger, chestnut and shiitake mushrooms and rice, then cook for 2 minutes, stirring, until the rice is coated and glossy.

3 Add the Chinese wine and cook for 3 minutes or until absorbed by the rice. Add a ladleful of hot stock, then stir continuously over a low heat with a wooden spoon until the rice has absorbed the liquid.

4 Continue to add the stock, a ladleful at a time, simmering until all the stock has been used and the rice is cooked and creamy but still retains a slight bite. Stir continuously to allow the rice to cook evenly and to prevent it from sticking to the bottom of the pan. This will take about 25 minutes.

5 Stir in the soy sauce and half of the coriander leaves and season with black pepper. Sprinkle with the chives and remaining coriander leaves and serve.

SUMMER PAELLA

This vegetarian version of the classic Spanish paella works brilliantly. The right type of rice – short-grain Calasparra – is essential, and the secret is to avoid stirring the rice during cooking so the base forms that desired golden crust. You can also serve this with a spoonful of Lemon and Garlic Mayonnaise (see page 138), if desired.

SERVES 4

55g/2oz/⅓ cup blanched almonds

150g/5 ½ oz/ 1 cup shelled broad beans

150g/5 ½ oz asparagus tips

½ tsp saffron strands

3 tbsp olive oil

2 onions, finely chopped

3 garlic cloves, chopped

1 large red pepper, deseeded and diced

1 tsp smoked paprika

1 tsp turmeric

375g/13oz/heaped 1⅔ cups Calasparra rice

80ml/2 ½ fl oz/⅓ cup dry sherry

900ml/31fl oz/3¾ cups vegetable stock

10 cherry tomatoes, halved

85g/3oz small black olives

basil leaves, to serve

salt and freshly ground black pepper

1 Toast the almonds in a dry frying pan over a medium heat for 3–4 minutes, stirring occasionally, until lightly browned. Then remove from the heat and set aside.

2 Blanch the broad beans in boiling water for 3 minutes until tender. Drain and refresh under cold running water, then gently squeeze the beans out of their outer skins into a bowl and set aside. Steam the asparagus for 3 minutes until just tender, refresh under cold running water and set aside. Put the saffron and 1 tablespoon hot water in a small bowl and set aside to infuse.

3 Heat the olive oil over a medium-low heat in a paella pan or large frying pan with a lid. Fry the onions, stirring regularly, for 5 minutes, then add the garlic and red pepper and fry, stirring occasionally, for another 3 minutes. Stir in the paprika, turmeric and rice and stir for 2 minutes until coated in the oil.

4 Add the sherry and cook until absorbed by the rice. Stir in the saffron with its soaking liquid and stock. Bring to the boil, stir, then reduce the heat to its lowest setting. Simmer for 20 minutes without stirring, until the stock is absorbed. Remove from the heat and top with the broad beans, cherry tomatoes, asparagus and olives. Set aside, covered, for 10 minutes to warm though.

5 Season with salt and pepper and serve topped with the almonds and basil.

DAL WITH TOASTED ALMONDS

SERVES 4–6

225g/8oz/1 cup red lentils
1 tbsp sunflower oil
1 tbsp mustard oil
1 large onion, finely chopped
3 garlic cloves, chopped
2.5cm/1in piece of root ginger,
  peeled and grated
2 tsp cumin seeds, ground
2 tsp mustard seeds, ground
12 curry leaves
2 tsp turmeric
5 tomatoes, peeled, deseeded and
  diced
3 small red chillies, slit open
  lengthways
1 tbsp tamarind paste
juice of 1 lime, plus wedges, to serve
2 tbsp toasted flaked almonds
salt and freshly ground black pepper

1 Put the lentils in a saucepan and cover with 800ml/28fl oz/scant 3½ cups water. Bring to the boil, then reduce the heat to low and simmer, partially covered, for 25–30 minutes until the lentils are very tender and they have absorbed the water.

2 Meanwhile, heat the sunflower and mustard oils in a large sauté pan over a medium-low heat and sauté the onion for 8 minutes until softened and golden. Add the garlic, ginger, cumin and mustard seeds, and curry leaves and cook, stirring, for 2 minutes.

3 Add the turmeric, tomatoes and chillies, reduce the heat to low and cook for 3 minutes until softened. Stir in the lentils, tamarind paste and lime juice, cover and warm through. Season with salt and pepper, top with the almonds and serve.

RED ONION CHUTNEY

SERVES 4

30g/1oz butter
2 tbsp olive oil
300g/10½ oz red onions, thinly
  sliced
50g/1¾ oz/heaped ¼ cup soft light
  brown sugar
100ml/3½ fl oz/scant ½ cup red
  wine
3 tbsp balsamic vinegar
salt and freshly ground black pepper

1 Heat the butter and olive oil in a heavy-based pan over a medium-low heat and cook the onions, stirring occasionally, for 15 minutes, partially covered, until softened. Add the muscovado sugar and cook over a low heat, stirring often, for another 15 minutes until caramelized.

2 Increase the heat to medium and add the red wine and vinegar – take care as it will spit a bit. Cook for 2 minutes, then reduce the heat to low. Simmer, partially covered, for 10–15 minutes or until reduced and thickened. Season with salt and pepper and leave to cool to room temperature before serving. Store in an airtight, sterilized jar in the fridge for up to 2 months.

PURPLE SPROUTING BROCCOLI WITH CHILLI, LEMON AND OLIVE OIL

SERVES 4

400g/14oz purple-sprouting broccoli
30g/1oz butter
2 tbsp lemon juice
finely grated zest of ½ lemon
1 medium red chilli, deseeded and
    finely chopped
salt

1 Boil the broccoli for 2 minutes, then refresh under cold running water and drain well.
2 Heat the butter in a frying pan over a medium-low heat and add the lemon juice, zest, and chilli. Stir well, then add the broccoli. Season with salt and warm through, turning briefly, until coated, then serve.

RICH ONION GRAVY

The perfect accompaniment to vegetarian pies and roasts. Cook the onions slowly until they are soft and their natural sugars start to caramelize.

SERVES 4

2 tbsp sunflower oil
2 onions, thinly sliced
2 tbsp plain flour
150ml/5fl oz/scant ⅔ cup dry red
    wine
350ml/12fl oz/scant 1½ cups
    vegetable stock
1 tbsp vegetarian Worcestershire
    sauce
1 tsp Dijon mustard
salt and freshly ground black pepper

1 Heat the sunflower oil in a saucepan over a medium-low heat and cook the onions for 12 minutes, stirring regularly, until light golden. Add the flour and cook, stirring continuously, for 1 minute.
2 Stir in the wine and bring to the boil, then reduce the heat to low and simmer for 3–5 minutes or until reduced by half.
3 Stir in the stock, Worcestershire sauce and Dijon mustard and simmer for 10 minutes until thickened. Season with salt and pepper and serve.

GLAZED HONEY AND ROSEMARY BABY CARROTS

SERVES 4

550g/1lb 4oz baby carrots, trimmed
30g/1oz butter
1 tbsp olive oil
1 large garlic clove, crushed
leaves from 2 rosemary sprigs,
    finely chopped
2 tsp wholegrain mustard
1 tbsp clear honey

1 Boil the carrots for 3 minutes until almost tender, then drain well.
2 Heat the butter and olive oil in a sauté pan over a medium-low heat. Add the garlic and rosemary and sauté for 1 minute, then add the carrots, mustard and honey. Cook over a low heat, stirring continuously to prevent the honey from burning, for 2 minutes until the carrots are tender and coated in the sticky glaze, then serve.

JEWELLED PERSIAN RICE

SERVES 4

250g/9oz/1¼ cups basmati rice
½ tsp salt, plus extra for seasoning
½ tsp saffron strands
2 tbsp olive oil
1 onion, finely chopped
1 courgette, diced
grated zest of 1 orange
1 tsp cumin seeds
1 tsp cinnamon
60g/2¼ oz/⅓ cup unsulphured
    dried apricots, chopped
55g/2oz/⅓ cup blanched almonds,
    chopped
35g/1¼ oz butter
3 tbsp dried barberries
freshly ground black pepper

1 If time allows, soak the rice for 1 hour, then drain and rinse under cold running water. Put the rice and salt in a saucepan and cover with water. Bring to the boil, then reduce the heat to low and simmer for 4 minutes. Drain again and set aside. Clean the pan.

2 Put the saffron and 4 tablespoons hot water in a small bowl and set aside to infuse. Meanwhile, heat half of the olive oil in a frying pan over a medium-low heat and fry the onion for 6 minutes, stirring occasionally, until softened. Add the courgette and cook for another 3 minutes, then stir in the orange zest, cumin seeds, cinnamon, dried apricots and almonds. Add the saffron and its soaking liquid, season with salt and pepper and mix well.

3 Heat the butter and remaining oil in the cleaned saucepan over a medium-low heat. When melted, add half of the rice and top with half of the vegetable mixture, then layer again with the rest of the rice and then the vegetable mixture. Using the handle of a wooden spoon, poke five holes into the rice and pour 1 teaspoon of boiling water into each. Cover with a tight-fitting lid and cook over a low heat for 10–15 minutes until the rice is tender and there is a light golden 'crust' on the bottom. Sprinkle with the barberries and serve.

PEAR CHUTNEY

SERVES 4

2 tbsp olive oil
1 onion, finely chopped
1 garlic clove, finely chopped
1 tsp ground cumin
1 tsp ground coriander
½ tsp ground mixed spice
80ml/2½ fl oz/⅓ cup red wine
    vinegar
50g/1¾ oz/heaped ¼ cup soft dark
    brown sugar
½ tsp salt
50g/1¾ oz/¼ cup unsulphured
    dried apricots, chopped
3 pears, peeled, cored and chopped

1 Heat the olive oil in a heavy-based saucepan over a medium-low heat and fry the onion for 6 minutes, stirring occasionally. Reduce the heat to low and fry, stirring occasionally, for another 6 minutes or until softened and golden in places.

2 Add the garlic and cook for 1 minute, then stir in all of the remaining ingredients and bring to the boil. Reduce the heat to low and simmer, covered, for 40 minutes until reduced and thickened. Stir occasionally to prevent the chutney from sticking. Leave to cool to room temperature before serving.

3 Store in an airtight, sterilised jar in the fridge for up to a month.

APPLE, BERRY AND PLUM PUDDING WITH ROSE CREAM

Similar to the classic British summer pudding, this delicious version features a rich, dark, fruity sauce and sweet brioche, and is made in layers rather than in a bowl.

SERVES 6

3 apples, peeled, cored and finely chopped

6 plums, halved, stoned and chopped

250ml/9fl oz/1 cup freshly squeezed orange juice

90g/3¼ oz/heaped ⅓ cup caster sugar

1 tsp cinnamon

½ tsp freshly grated nutmeg

½ tsp ground ginger

300g/10½ oz/heaped 2½ cups blackberries

400g/14oz brioche loaf, sliced and crusts removed (optional)

ROSE CREAM

200ml/7fl oz/scant 1 cup whipping cream

2 tbsp icing sugar

1 tsp rosewater

1 Put the apples, plums, orange juice, caster sugar, cinnamon, nutmeg and ginger in a saucepan and bring to the boil. Reduce the heat to low and simmer, partially covered, for 8 minutes. Add the blackberries and cook for another 4–8 minutes until the fruit is tender. Strain the cooking juice into a jug and set aside.

2 Arrange half of the brioche slices in a single layer in a 25 x 20cm/ 10 x 8in dish. Top with the cooked fruit and pour some of the strained juice over the top so the bread is ruby red.

3 Put a second layer of brioche on top of the fruit and pour enough of the cooking juice over to soak the bread, but do not allow it to become too soggy – you will still have some juice left over. Press a sheet of greaseproof paper over the top of the bread and weight down with a plate. Chill for at least 3 hours or overnight. Chill the reserved cooking juice until ready to serve.

4 To make the rose cream, whisk the cream in a clean bowl until it forms soft peaks. Gradually whisk in the icing sugar and then stir in the rosewater. Cover and chill until required.

5 Cut the pudding into 6 portions and serve topped with a spoonful of the rose cream and drizzled with the reserved cooking juice.

HOME-MADE CRÈME FRAÎCHE WITH CHERRY COMPÔTE

Making your own crème fraîche is fun and easy, but you do need to plan ahead. The rich, velvety, slightly sour cream will keep for a couple of weeks in the fridge.

SERVES 4
250ml/9fl oz/1 cup double cream
1 heaped tbsp buttermilk

CHERRY COMPÔTE
680g/1lb 8oz cherries
70g/2½ oz/scant ⅓ cup caster
    sugar
2 tbsp kirsch or brandy
2 tsp cornflour

1 Gently warm the cream in a saucepan over a medium-low heat to 40°C/105°F. Remove from the heat and pour into a clean glass jar. Stir in the buttermilk until well combined, then cover with cling film or greaseproof paper and secure with a rubber band.

2 Put the jar in a warm draft-free place and leave to thicken — this will take anything from 12 to 24 hours. Once thickened, stir well, cover with a lid and chill. The crème fraîche is ready to eat now but it will continue to thicken. Store, covered, in the fridge for up to 2 weeks. Serve chilled — it should have a slightly nutty, sour taste.

3 To make the cherry compôte, put the cherries, caster sugar and 2 tablespoons water in a saucepan and simmer for 2 minutes, stirring to dissolve the sugar. Mix together the kirsch and cornflour, then gradually stir the mixture into the cherries. Continue simmering for another 2–3 minutes or until thickened. Serve with the crème fraîche.

JASMINE TEA AND GINGER PEARS

These pears are poached in fragrant Jasmine tea that's flavoured with aromatic ginger and star anise. Choose pears that are slightly under-ripe to prevent them from becoming too soft during poaching.

SERVES 4
4 slightly under-ripe pears
1 tbsp lemon juice
3 Jasmine tea bags
8 slices of root ginger
1 cinnamon stick
4 tbsp caster sugar
3 star anise

1 Peel and halve the pears and, using a melon baller or teaspoon, scoop out the cores. Coat in the lemon juice to prevent them from discolouring.

2 Bring 875ml/30fl oz/3½ cups water to the boil in a large sauté pan. Reduce the heat to medium, add the Jasmine tea bags and simmer for 5 minutes, then remove the tea bags from the pan.

3 Add the pears, ginger, cinnamon, caster sugar and star anise and simmer, partially covered, for 15–20 minutes until tender. Using a slotted spoon, remove the pears from the pan. Increase the heat to medium-high and cook for 2–3 minutes until the cooking liquid has reduced and thickened. Remove and discard the spices. Serve 2 pear halves per person with the syrup spooned over the tops.

SPICED CHOCOLATE MOUSSE WITH NUT BRITTLE

SERVES 4

100g/3½ oz dark chocolate, about 70% cocoa solids, broken into even-sized pieces

2 large eggs, separated

150ml/5fl oz/scant ⅔ cup double cream

4 tbsp caster sugar

1 tsp ground allspice

½ tsp cinnamon

NUT BRITTLE

150g/5½ oz/heaped ⅔ cup granulated sugar

80g/2¾ oz/½ cup roasted salted peanuts, coarsely chopped

40g/1½ oz butter

1 To make the nut brittle, line a baking sheet with baking parchment. Dissolve the granulated sugar in a saucepan over a low heat, stirring occasionally, until light golden. Stir in the peanuts and butter and, when the butter has melted, pour the mixture on to the baking sheet. Leave to cool and harden, then break into pieces.

2 Put the chocolate in a heatproof bowl and rest it over a pan of gently simmering water, making sure the bottom of the bowl does not touch the water. Heat for 4–5 minutes, stirring, until the chocolate has melted, then set aside to cool slightly.

3 Whisk the egg yolks and a large spoonful of the cream into the melted chocolate. In a large, clean bowl, whisk the egg whites until they form soft peaks. Gradually whisk in the caster sugar, allspice and cinnamon until glossy soft peaks form.

4 Whisk the cream until it forms soft peaks. Fold the chocolate mixture into the cream, followed by the egg white mixture. Spoon into four small pots or teacups and chill for 1 hour or until set. Serve each chocolate mousse with a piece of the nut brittle.

LEMON POSSET WITH SESAME FILO CRISPS

SERVES 4

420ml/14½ fl oz/1⅔ cups double cream

140g/5oz/⅔ cup caster sugar

70ml/2¼ fl oz/scant ⅓ cup lemon juice

finely grated zest of 1 small lemon

FILO CRISPS

1 filo sheet, about 50 x 24cm/ 20 x 9½ in

30g/1oz butter, melted

2 tbsp maple syrup

1 tbsp sesame seeds

1 To make the filo crisps, preheat the oven to 200°C/400°F/gas 6 and line a baking sheet with baking parchment. Lay out the filo sheet on a work surface and cut it in half lengthways, then cut each half into quarters. Brush each piece with melted butter and fold over lengthways twice to make a 1.5cm/⅝in stick. Brush the tops with the maple syrup and sprinkle with the sesame seeds. Bake for 10 minutes until crisp and light golden, then remove from the oven and leave to cool.

2 Put the cream and caster sugar in a saucepan and bring to the boil, stirring regularly, until the sugar is dissolved. Reduce the heat to low and simmer for 5 minutes, stirring occasionally, until it is thick enough to coat the back of a spoon.

3 Remove from the heat and stir in the lemon juice and zest. Pour the mixture into four espresso cups or small glasses. The possets can either be served warm or chilled for about 1 hour until set. Serve each lemon posset with 2 sesame filo crisps.

RICE PUDDING WITH APRICOTS IN CARDAMOM SYRUP

SERVES 4
200g/7oz/scant 1 cup pudding rice
625ml/21½ fl oz/2½ cups milk
2 tsp cinnamon
1 tsp freshly grated nutmeg
6 tbsp caster sugar
finely grated zest of 1 large orange
3 tbsp single cream
4 tbsp toasted flaked almonds

APRICOTS IN CARDAMOM SYRUP
300g/10½ oz/2 cups dried
   unsulphured apricots
5 cardamom pods, lightly crushed
3 tbsp clear honey

1 Put the apricots, cardamom, honey and 375ml/13fl oz/1½ cups water in a saucepan and stir well. Bring to the boil, then reduce the heat to low and simmer, partially covered, for 20 minutes until the apricots are plump and tender and the sauce has become syrupy. Remove from the heat and set aside.

2 Meanwhile, put the rice and 600ml/21fl oz/scant 2½ cups water in a heavy-based saucepan. Bring to the boil, then reduce the heat to low and simmer, uncovered, for 15 minutes or until the water is absorbed.

3 Stir in the milk, cinnamon, nutmeg, caster sugar and orange zest and bring to the boil again. Reduce the heat to low and simmer, partially covered, for 20 minutes, stirring regularly, or until the rice is cooked. Stir in the cream and gently heat through.

4 Divide the rice pudding into bowls, sprinkle with the almonds and serve with the apricots and syrup.

ZABAGLIONE WITH RHUBARB COMPÔTE

SERVES 4
4 egg yolks
55g/2oz/¼ cup caster sugar
5 tbsp Marsala wine

RHUBARB COMPÔTE
300g/10½ oz rhubarb, thickly sliced
½ tsp vanilla extract
4 tbsp caster sugar, plus extra as
   needed

1 To make the compôte, put the rhubarb, vanilla extract, caster sugar and 2 tablespoons water in a saucepan. Bring to the boil, then reduce the heat to low and simmer for 7 minutes or until very tender. Taste and add more sugar, if desired, remembering that the zabaglione is sweet. Remove from the heat and set aside.

2 Put the egg yolks and caster sugar in a heatproof bowl and rest it over a pan of simmering water, making sure the bottom of the bowl does not touch the water. Whisk beat until the mixture is pale and the texture resembles double cream. Slowly add the Marsala wine and continue whisking for about 15 minutes, until the mixture has almost tripled in volume and become light, frothy and creamy.

3 Divide half of the rhubarb compôte into four glasses, then top with half of the zabaglione, followed by the rest of the compôte and zabaglione. Swirl with a spoon to give a marbled effect, then serve immediately or chill until ready to eat.

CHOCOLATE, GINGER, ALMOND AND CHERRY SLAB

SERVES 8

60g/2¼oz/heaped ⅓ cup blanched
   almonds
300g/10½oz dark chocolate, about
   70% cocoa solids, broken into
   even-sized pieces
35g/1¼oz preserved ginger,
   drained and coarsely chopped
55g/2oz/¼ cup dried sour cherries
165g/5¾oz white chocolate, broken
   into even-sized chunks

1 Line a square 15cm/6in baking tin with cling film. Toast the almonds in a dry frying pan over a medium heat for 3–4 minutes, stirring occasionally, until lightly browned, then set aside.

2 Put the dark chocolate in a heatproof bowl and rest it over a pan of gently simmering water, making sure the bottom of the bowl does not touch the water. Heat for 4–5 minutes, stirring, until the chocolate has melted. Carefully remove the bowl from the heat and stir in the ginger, cherries and almonds. Pour the mixture into the prepared tin and spread into an even layer.

3 Melt the white chocolate, following the same instructions as in step 2 for the dark chocolate. Dot spoonfuls of the melted white chocolate on top of the dark chocolate and, using a skewer, swirl the chocolates together to make a marble pattern.

4 Put the chocolate slab in the fridge and chill for 1 hour or until set. Break into large chunks and store in an airtight container in the fridge until ready to eat.

ESPRESSO POTS WITH CARAMELIZED COFFEE SAUCE

SERVES 6

250ml/9fl oz/1 cup double cream
250ml/9fl oz/1 cup milk
1 tsp vanilla extract
2 tbsp brewed espresso coffee
3 eggs
70g/2½oz/scant ⅓ cup caster
   sugar

CARAMELIZED COFFEE SAUCE
200g/7oz/scant 1 cup caster sugar
100ml/3½fl oz/scant ½ cup
   brewed espresso coffee
30g/1oz butter

1 Preheat the oven to 160°C/315°F/gas 3. To make the caramelized coffee sauce, put the caster sugar in a heavy-based saucepan over a medium heat and cook, stirring occasionally, for 5 minutes or until it has melted and turned a rich golden brown. Remove from the heat and stir in the coffee, taking care as it will froth up – it is a good idea to wear an oven glove. Return to a low heat, stir until combined and smooth, then stir in the butter. Remove from the heat and set aside.

2 Gently heat the cream, milk, vanilla extract and coffee in a saucepan over a medium-low heat until just below the boil, then remove from the heat and leave to cool slightly.

3 Meanwhile, whisk together the eggs and caster sugar, then stir in the cream mixture. Divide into six 150ml/5fl oz/scant ⅔ cup ramekins or ovenproof glasses and put them in a baking dish. Add enough water to the dish to come halfway up the sides of the ramekins and bake for 25 minutes or until just set (they will still be quite wobbly). Carefully remove from the dish, leave to cool at room temperature for 15 minutes and then chill until set.

4 Pour some of the caramelized coffee sauce over each espresso pot and serve.

More than with any other method of cooking, baking cleverly lets you know when foods are ready by releasing a tantalizing aroma that's impossible to ignore. From colourful vegetable tarts and golden pies to sumptuous cakes and roasted fruits, these recipes are full of stunning flavors.

BAKE

Roasted Balsamic Pears, page 222

INDIAN-STYLE PANZANELLA

This dish incorporates all the elements associated with the rustic Italian bread salad but comes with an Indian twist. Paneer is a semi-hard, mild-tasting Indian cheese and is now readily available sold in blocks in Asian stores or supermarkets.

SERVES 4

6 tbsp balti or other curry paste
2 tbsp sunflower oil, plus extra for greasing and deep-frying
300g/10½ oz paneer cheese, cut into 12 slices
150g/5½ oz/heaped 1 cup cooked chickpeas
2 small naan breads, split open
250g/9oz cherry tomatoes, halved
1 small cucumber, quartered lengthways, deseeded and cut into small chunks
1 small red onion, sliced into thin rings
1 small fennel bulb, thinly sliced
juice of 1 lime
4 uncooked poppadoms
125ml/4fl oz/½ cup natural yogurt
1 garlic clove, crushed
1 tsp cumin seeds
salt and freshly ground black pepper
mint leaves, to serve

1 Mix together the curry paste and sunflower oil in a shallow dish. Add the paneer and turn to coat in the mixture, then set aside to marinate for 1 hour.

2 Preheat the oven to 180°C/350°F/gas 4 and lightly grease a large baking sheet with oil. Using a slotted spoon, remove the paneer from the marinade and put it on the baking sheet. Add the chickpeas to the marinade and turn until coated, then transfer to the baking sheet. Roast the paneer and chickpeas for 20–25 minutes, turning occasionally, until the paneer is golden and the chickpeas are slightly crisp.

3 Meanwhile, put the naan bread on a baking sheet and bake for 5–8 minutes until crisp. Leave to cool, then break into bite-sized pieces.

4 Put the tomatoes, cucumber, onion and fennel in a bowl, add half of the lime juice and season with salt and pepper. Toss well.

5 Heat 5cm/2in of the sunflower oil in a wide saucepan over a medium-high heat until it reaches 190°C/375°F. A cube of bread will turn golden in 20 seconds when dropped into the oil. Cook the poppadoms, one at a time, for 2–3 seconds each, holding them under the oil with a spatula until puffed up and crisp. Drain on kitchen paper.

6 Mix together the yogurt, garlic and remaining lime juice in a bowl. Season with salt and pepper, then sprinkle with the cumin seeds.

7 Put 1 poppadom on each of four plates and top with the tomato salad. Scatter the chickpeas and naan bread over the salad, then top with the paneer and a large spoonful of the yogurt mixture. Sprinkle with a few mint leaves and serve.

LINGUINE BAKED IN PAPER

The paper parcels keep in all those lovely juices and the flavour of the herbs, wine, tomatoes and garlic, which infuse the pasta during baking. There's no need to remove the paper after cooking as it adds to its presentation.

SERVES 4

380g/13½ oz linguine

2 tbsp olive oil

2 large garlic cloves, finely chopped

1 long red chilli, deseeded and finely chopped

200ml/7 floz/scant 1 cup dry white wine

440g/15½ oz cherry tomatoes

3 tbsp small capers, drained and rinsed

3 tbsp chopped flat-leaf parsley leaves

salt and freshly ground black pepper

Parmesan cheese shavings, to serve

1 Cook the pasta in plenty of boiling salted water until almost cooked, about 10 minutes, then drain, reserving 2 tablespoons of the cooking water.

2 Meanwhile, heat the olive oil in a frying pan and fry the garlic and chilli for 1 minute, stirring occasionally. Add the wine and bring to the boil, then reduce the heat slightly and cook for 3–5 minutes until the wine is reduced by about one-third and the alcohol is burnt off.

3 Preheat the oven to 180°C/350°F/gas 4. Add the tomatoes and capers to the frying pan and cook, stirring occasionally, for 3 minutes until softened slightly. Add the pasta, reserved cooking water and parsley. Remove from the heat and stir until the pasta is coated in the sauce.

4 Put a large sheet of baking paper in each of four bowls and divide the pasta into them. Gather up the edges of the paper and tie with kitchen string, then put the parcels on a baking sheet and bake for 15 minutes. To serve, return the parcels to the bowls and open carefully. Sprinkle with Parmesan, season with black pepper and serve.

ITALIAN BAKED LEMONS WITH MOZZARELLA

SERVES 4

3 large lemons

12 large basil leaves

3 x 125g/4½ oz mozzarella balls,
    drained, patted dry and cut into
    12 slices

12 sun-blush tomatoes in oil,
    drained

salt and freshly ground black pepper

1 Slice off and discard the ends of the lemons, then cut each one into 4 slices, each about 1cm/½ in thick. Using a sharp knife, cut around and remove the flesh (saving it for another use) so you are left with 12 rings of lemon peel. Preheat the oven to 180°C/350°F/gas 4 and line a large baking sheet with baking paper.

2 Put each lemon ring on each basil leaf and arrange on the baking sheet. Press 1 slice of mozzarella into each ring and top with 1 sun-blush tomato. Bake for 8–10 minutes until the mozzarella is slightly melted and heated through —it shouldn't be allowed to get too soft or it will seep out of its shell. Season with salt and pepper and serve warm.

ROASTED ROOT VEGETABLE SOUP

Roasting the vegetables enhances their natural sweetness, adding a depth of flavour to this hearty soup. Feel free to adapt the root vegetables depending on what you have to hand and what is in season.

SERVES 4–6

1 small winter squash, such as
    butternut, kabocha or pumpkin,
    peeled, deseeded and cut into
    bite-sized chunks

2 parsnips, cut into 1cm/½ in
    rounds

2 carrots, cut into 1cm/½ in rounds

2 onions, peeled and quartered

1 swede, peeled and cut into
    bite-sized chunks

1 garlic bulb, top trimmed

3 tbsp olive oil

4 long rosemary sprigs

a few sprigs thyme

1.5l/52fl oz/6 cups vegetable stock

2 bay leaves

salt and freshly ground black pepper

soured cream, to serve

1 Preheat the oven to 200°C/400°F/gas 6. Put the squash, parsnips, carrots, onions, swede and garlic in a large bowl. Drizzle the olive oil over them, season with salt and pepper and then toss until evenly coated. Spread the vegetables out in a single layer in two baking trays and add the rosemary and thyme. Bake for 25 minutes, then remove the garlic bulb and herbs and return the remaining vegetables to the oven, swapping the trays around. Bake for another 20–25 minutes until tender.

2 Squeeze the soft garlic out of each clove and put it in a large saucepan. Add the roasted vegetables, stock and bay leaves and bring to the boil over a high heat. Reduce the heat to low and simmer for 10–15 minutes until the vegetables are very tender. Remove and discard the bay leaves, then blend the soup until smooth and thick, adding more stock if necessary.

3 Reheat the soup, if necessary, taste and season again with salt and pepper, if desired. Divide into bowls, top with a swirl of soured cream and serve.

ROASTED SWEET POTATO AND SMOKED TOFU SALAD

SERVES 4

4 tbsp black bean sauce

2 tbsp light soy sauce

1 tsp sunflower oil, plus extra for
  greasing

3 tsp sesame oil

225g/8oz smoked tofu, cut into
  bite-sized cubes

2 sweet potatoes, peeled and cut
  into bite-sized cubes

2 tbsp pumpkin seeds

4 romaine lettuce leaves, shredded

100g/3½ oz red cabbage, shredded

½ red onion, finely chopped

3 tbsp olive oil

2 tbsp lemon juice

1 handful of broccoli sprouts, to
  serve

salt and freshly ground black pepper

1 Mix together the black bean sauce, soy sauce, sunflower oil and
  1 teaspoon of the sesame oil in a shallow dish. Add the tofu, turn to
  coat in the marinade, then set aside to marinate for at least
  30 minutes.

2 Preheat the oven to 190°C/375°F/gas 5 and lightly grease two
  baking sheets with sunflower oil. Put the tofu on one of the baking
  sheets and bake for 20–25 minutes, turning once, until golden all
  over. At the same time, put the sweet potato on the other baking
  sheet, turn to coat in the oil and season with salt and pepper. Roast
  for 20–25 minutes, turning once, until tender and golden.

3 Meanwhile, toast the pumpkin seeds in a dry frying pan over a
  medium heat for 3–4 minutes, stirring occasionally, until lightly
  browned, then remove from the heat and set aside.

4 Divide the lettuce, cabbage and red onion into four large, shallow
  bowls. Mix together the olive oil, lemon juice and remaining sesame
  oil and season with salt and pepper. Drizzle the dressing over the
  salad and top with the roasted sweet potatoes and tofu. Sprinkle
  with the toasted pumpkin seeds and broccoli sprouts, then serve.

TIAN OF SUMMER VEGETABLES

SERVES 4

6 tbsp olive oil, plus extra for
  drizzling

1 aubergine, cut into 5mm/¼ in
  rounds

1 large onion, thinly sliced

2 garlic cloves, chopped

2 red peppers, deseeded and sliced

1 large handful of basil leaves

250g/9oz mozzarella balls, drained
  and sliced

2 courgettes, sliced diagonally

2 tomatoes, sliced

20g/¾ oz butter

6 tbsp fresh breadcrumbs

1 red chilli, deseeded and chopped

4 tbsp grated Parmesan cheese

salt and freshly ground black pepper

1 Heat 2 tablespoons of the olive oil in a large frying pan. Fry half of
  the aubergine for 4 minutes on each side until softened and slightly
  golden. Remove from the pan with a slotted spoon and arrange in
  a single layer in a 26 x 20cm/10½ x 8in ovenproof baking dish.
  Repeat with the remaining aubergine, adding a little more oil if
  necessary. Add the onion to the pan and fry, stirring occasionally,
  for 8 minutes until softened. Add the garlic and cook for 2 minutes.

2 Preheat the oven to 200°C/400°F/gas 6. Top the aubergine with a
  layer of peppers, half of the basil and half of the mozzarella. Spread
  the onion and garlic over the cheese and arrange the courgettes
  in an even layer on top. Layer again with the remaining basil
  and mozzarella, then with the tomatoes. Drizzle with olive oil,
  season with salt and pepper and bake for 35–45 minutes until the
  vegetables are cooked and the mozzarella is bubbling.

3 Meanwhile, melt the butter in a frying pan, then fry the breadcrumbs
  for 5 minutes until light golden. Add the chilli, cook for 1 minute, then
  remove from the heat and stir in the Parmesan. Sprinkle the mixture
  over the tian and serve.

BLACK OLIVE FARINATA WITH SPINACH TZATZIKI

Farinata is a type of Italian pancake made with chickpea flour. Variations exist in North Africa and South America.

SERVES 4

150g/5½oz/1⅓ cups chickpea flour

½ tsp salt

1 large egg, lightly beaten

5 tbsp olive oil

50g/1¾oz/heaped ⅓ cup pitted black olives, halved

1 heaped tbsp chopped rosemary

1 red onion, thinly sliced into rounds

1 red chilli, deseeded and thinly sliced

salt and freshly ground black pepper

SPINACH TZATZIKI

170ml/5½fl oz/⅔ cup natural yogurt

1 small garlic clove, chopped

250g/9oz spinach leaves, tough stalks removed

squeeze of lemon juice

1 Put the chickpea flour and salt in a bowl and make a well in the centre. Add the egg, 2 tablespoons of the olive oil and 400ml/ 14fl oz/scant 1⅔ cups lukewarm water. Using a wooden spoon, gradually draw the flour into the wet ingredients and stir to make a thick, smooth batter, then cover and leave to rest for 1 hour.

2 Meanwhile, make the spinach tzatziki. Mix together the yogurt, garlic and 4 tablespoons water. Steam the spinach for 2 minutes or until wilted, then drain well and press the spinach with the back of a wooden spoon to squeeze out any excess water. Unravel the spinach and mix it into the yogurt mixture. Stir in a squeeze of lemon juice, season with salt and pepper and chill until needed.

3 Preheat the oven to 220°C/425°F/gas 7. Pour the remaining oil into a 33 x 23cm/13 x 9in baking tray and heat in the oven for 2–3 minutes until very hot, then carefully remove from the oven. While the oil is heating, skim any froth off the top of the farinata batter and stir well.

4 Carefully pour the batter into the baking tray and sprinkle the olives, rosemary, onion and chilli over the top and bake for 15–20 minutes or until set and golden. Cut into squares and serve warm with the tzatziki.

BAKED EGGS IN FILO WITH TOMATO PICKLE AND GARLIC MUSHROOMS

Filo pastry makes simple and pretty individual pastry cases. When using filo it is important not to let it dry out, so keep the unused pastry covered with a clean, slightly damp tea towel while you work.

SERVES 4
70g/2½oz butter, melted
4 large sheets filo pastry
8 eggs

TOMATO PICKLE
2 tsp olive oil
1 onion, finely chopped
5 tomatoes, deseeded and chopped
1 tsp Dijon mustard
4 tbsp white wine vinegar
2 tbsp soft light brown sugar
salt and freshly ground black pepper

GARLIC MUSHROOMS
2 tbsp olive oil
butter, melted
250g/9oz chestnut mushrooms, sliced
3 garlic cloves, finely chopped
1 tbsp chopped parsley leaves

1 First make the tomato pickle. Heat the olive oil in a pan over a medium-low heat and fry the onion for 8 minutes, stirring occasionally, until softened. Add the tomatoes, mustard, vinegar and brown sugar, and season with salt and pepper. Bring to the boil, then reduce the heat to low and simmer, partially covered, for 10–15 minutes, until thickened. Transfer to a serving bowl.

2 Preheat the oven to 200°C/400°F/gas 6 and brush 8 holes of a deep muffin tin with a little of the melted butter. Lay the filo sheets on top of one another and cut them in half crossways, then cut each half into 4 squares. Take one square and brush a little butter between each layer of filo, then press it into a muffin hole to make a basket shape. Repeat with the remaining filo to make 8 baskets and brush the overhanging pastry (but not the inside) with a little more butter. Break 1 egg into each filo basket, season with salt and pepper and bake for 12–15 minutes until the eggs are just set and the pastry is golden.

3 While the eggs are baking, make the garlic mushrooms. Put the olive oil and butter into a frying pan and fry the mushrooms for 5 minutes until tender. Add the garlic, season with salt and pepper and fry for another 2 minutes, then sprinkle with the parsley. Top the eggs with the mushrooms and serve with the tomato pickle.

CAULIFLOWER AND CHEESE CUSTARDS WITH ROASTED TOMATOES

Cheese and cauliflower are a classic combination and here they are turned into light savoury puddings. Roasting intensifies the flavour of the tomatoes and the combination of brown sugar, balsamic vinegar and harissa gives them a slightly caramelized, spicy stickiness.

SERVES 4

1 small cauliflower, cut into small florets
100ml/3½ fl oz/scant ½ cup milk
4 eggs
4 tbsp crème fraîche
125g/4½ oz/heaped 1 cup grated mature Cheddar cheese
salt and freshly ground black pepper
8 thick slices of toasted crusty bread, to serve

ROASTED TOMATOES

2 tbsp olive oil, plus extra for greasing
2 tbsp balsamic vinegar
½ –1 tsp harissa paste, to taste
12 tomatoes, halved lengthways
1 tsp soft dark brown sugar
1 heaped tsp coriander seeds, crushed

1 To make the roasted tomatoes, preheat the oven to 180°C/350°F/gas 4, line a baking tray with foil and grease lightly. Mix together the olive oil, balsamic vinegar and harissa in a shallow dish and season with salt and pepper. Add the tomatoes and turn until coated, then arrange them, cut-side up, on the baking tray. Sprinkle with the brown sugar and coriander seeds and bake for 50–55 minutes until soft and slightly caramelized.

2 Meanwhile, steam the cauliflower for 5 minutes until tender. Transfer to a blender, add the milk and purée until smooth. In a mixing bowl, whisk together the eggs and crème fraîche, then stir in the Cheddar and cauliflower purée. Season with salt and pepper, then divide the mixture into four 185ml/6fl oz/¾ cup ramekins arranged on a baking tray.

3 After the tomatoes have been cooking for 30 minutes, put the baking tray in the oven and bake the custards alongside the tomatoes for 20–25 minutes until set and risen.

4 Serve the cauliflower custards with the roasted tomatoes and toasted bread.

CHAR SUI TEMPEH WITH CHINESE PANCAKES

Tempeh is made from fermented soya beans and has a firm texture and nutty, mushroomy flavour. Like tofu, which is also made from soya beans, it benefits from marinating and readily takes on the flavour of stronger ingredients.

SERVES 4

350g/12oz tempeh
5 tbsp hoisin sauce
3 tbsp light soy sauce
1 tsp sunflower oil
3 tbsp clear honey
1 tsp Chinese five-spice powder
8 Chinese pancakes
1 small cucumber, deseeded and cut into strips
3 spring onions, thinly sliced lengthways into strips
1 red chilli, deseeded and thinly sliced
8 large basil leaves

1. Steam the tempeh for 5 minutes until softened – this also helps to remove any trace of bitterness.
2. Mix together the hoisin sauce, soy sauce, sunflower oil, honey and Chinese five-spice in a shallow dish. Add the tempeh, turn to coat in the marinade and then leave to marinate for 1 hour. Preheat the oven to 200°C/400°F/gas 6.
3. Loosely wrap the tempeh in foil and put it in a roasting tray, reserving any leftover marinade. Bake for 15 minutes, then remove from the oven. Preheat the grill to medium-high.
4. Carefully remove the tempeh from the oven and unwrap. Pour off and reserve any cooking juices in the foil and return the tempeh to the roasting tray. Spoon some of the marinade over the tempeh and grill for 5 minutes until golden and glossy, turning halfway and spooning more of the marinade over the tempeh. Slice the tempeh into long strips. Combine any leftover marinade with the reserved cooking juices.
5. Meanwhile, wrap the Chinese pancakes in foil and heat them for 3–4 minutes in the still-warm oven. Put the pancakes on plates and divide the tempeh over them. Top each one with a spoonful of the marinade, then the cucumber, spring onions, chilli and basil. Roll up the pancakes or serve flat.

MUSHROOM AND CASHEW PIES WITH RED ONION CHUTNEY

There's something very appealing about an individual pie. They make a hearty Sunday lunch served with Rich Onion Gravy (see page 179), and their portable size means they're great for picnics, too.

SERVES 4

20g/¾ oz dried porcini mushrooms
2 tbsp olive oil
2 onions, finely chopped
3 garlic cloves, finely chopped
250g/9oz chestnut mushrooms,
    coarsely chopped
2 tsp dried thyme
3 tbsp sherry
1 tbsp dark soy sauce
125g/4½ oz/heaped 1 cup broken
    cashew nuts
80g/2¾ oz/scant 1 cup fresh
    breadcrumbs
50g/1¾ oz/scant ½ cup ground
    almonds
egg, for glazing
salt and freshly ground black pepper
1 recipe quantity Red Onion Chutney
    (see page 178), to serve

PASTRY

225g/8oz/ 1¾ cups plain flour, plus
    extra for rolling the pastry
½ tsp salt
60g/2¼ oz cold butter, diced, plus
    extra for greasing
1 egg yolk

1 First make the pastry. Sift the flour and salt into a bowl. Rub in the butter with your fingertips until the mixture resembles fine breadcrumbs. Add the egg yolk and a little cold water, if necessary, and mix to combine; press the dough together to make a smooth ball, wrap in cling film and chill for 30 minutes.

2 Meanwhile, put the porcini mushrooms in a small bowl and just cover with boiling water; leave to soak for 20 minutes. Strain them, reserving 3 tablespoons of the soaking liquid, then roughly chop.

3 Heat the olive oil over a medium-low heat and fry the onions, stirring occasionally, for 15−20 minutes, partially covered, until golden and very soft. Add the garlic, porcini and chestnut mushrooms and thyme and fry, uncovered, for 5 minutes, stirring occasionally. Add the sherry, soy sauce and reserved mushroom liquid and simmer for 2 minutes or until the liquid has reduced by half.

4 Finely grind the cashews in a food processor. Transfer to a large bowl and stir in the breadcrumbs and almonds. Put the mushroom mixture in the food processor and process to a smooth paste, then add to the cashews. Season with salt and pepper and stir until well combined and the mixture has the consistency of a firm pâté.

5 Preheat the oven to 200°C/400°F/gas 6. Grease four 150ml/5fl oz/ scant ⅔ cup dariole moulds. Roll out the pastry on a lightly floured work surface and cut out 4 circles to line the moulds, gathering up the trimmings. Put 1 circle in each mould and press it from the bottom upwards to get rid of any air bubbles and shape it into a pastry case. Leave 2cm/¾ in of the pastry overhanging the top of the mould.

6 Fill the pastry cases nearly to the top with the mushroom mixture. Re-roll the pastry trimmings and cut out 4 circles to fit as lids on top of the moulds. Wet the edge of each pastry case with water and press the lid on the top, pinching with your fingers to seal. Trim any excess pastry.

7 Brush the tops with egg, put the pies on a baking sheet and bake for 35−40 minutes until golden. Leave to rest for 2−3 minutes before loosening the pies with a knife and carefully turning them out. Serve hot with chutney.

RED ONION, BEETROOT AND GOAT'S CHEESE TART

The walnut pastry in this tart complements the earthy quality of the beetroot as well as the slight sweetness of the red onions and goat's cheese. If time allows, boil or roast the beetroot or, alternatively, use ready-cooked beetroot – but make sure to choose ones in natural juice rather than pickled in vinegar.

SERVES 4–6

1 tbsp olive oil

25g/1oz unsalted butter, plus extra for greasing

680g/1lb 8oz red onions, thinly sliced

5 thyme sprigs, plus extra to serve

3 tbsp balsamic vinegar

400g/14oz cooked baby beetroot, halved lengthways

1 tbsp clear honey

1 x 175g/6oz goat's cheese round, crumbled

salt and freshly ground black pepper

WALNUT PASTRY

40g/1½oz/scant ½ cup walnuts

185g/6½oz/1½ cups plain flour, sifted, plus extra for rolling the pastry

85g/3oz cold butter, diced

1 egg, separated

1 To make the pastry, toast the walnuts in a dry frying pan over a medium heat for 4–5 minutes, turning occasionally, until light golden, then chop finely and set aside. Put the flour, a generous pinch of salt and butter in a food processor and pulse until it resembles fine breadcrumbs. Add the walnuts, egg yolk and 2–3 tablespoons cold water and continue to pulse until the mixture forms a ball of dough. Remove the dough from the food processor, wrap in cling film and chill for 30 minutes.

2 Meanwhile, heat the oil and butter in a large sauté pan and fry the onions over a low heat, partially covered, for 20 minutes, stirring occasionally, until softened but not coloured. Add the thyme and balsamic vinegar and cook for another 5 minutes until the vinegar has been absorbed. Add the beetroot and honey and stir until glossy, then season with salt and pepper and set aside.

3 Preheat the oven to 180°C/350°F/gas 4 and lightly grease a 24cm/9½in loose-bottomed flan tin with butter. Roll out the pastry on a lightly floured work surface and gently press it into the prepared tin. Prick the pastry case a few times with a fork, then line it with baking paper and fill with baking beans. Bake for 20 minutes until almost cooked, then remove the beans and paper and bake for another 15 minutes until cooked.

4 Brush the pastry shell with beaten egg white and fill with the onion and beetroot mixture. Arrange the goat's cheese on top and bake for 15 minutes, until the cheese has browned in places. Decorate with a few sprigs of thyme and serve.

BAKED TOMATO RISOTTO WITH WINTER PESTO AND PARMESAN–WALNUT CRISPS

This risotto goes against the grain: it's baked in the oven rather than cooked on the hob, and conveniently only needs to be stirred once. Topped with a spoonful of the aromatic winter herb pesto and a feather-light Parmesan crisp, it's comfort food at its most perfect.

SERVES 4

40g/1½oz/scant ½ cup halved walnuts

4 heaped tbsp grated Parmesan cheese, plus extra, shaved, to serve

2 tbsp olive oil

30g/1oz butter

2 onions, finely chopped

3 garlic cloves, finely chopped

300g/10½oz/1⅓ cups risotto rice

185ml/6fl oz/¾ cup dry red wine

500ml/17fl oz/2 cups hot vegetable stock

500ml/17fl oz/2 cups passata

1 heaped tsp sun-dried tomato paste

salt and freshly ground black pepper

WINTER PESTO

15g/½oz mixed herbs, including sage, rosemary and thyme

1 garlic clove

6 tbsp olive oil

4 heaped tbsp grated Parmesan cheese

1 Preheat the oven to 180°C/350°F/gas 4. Put the walnuts on a baking sheet and bake for 3–4 minutes until lightly toasted. Remove from the oven and leave to cool slightly, then finely chop half of the walnuts and set the rest aside.

2 To make the Parmesan crisps, line the baking sheet with baking paper. Sprinkle 1 tablespoon of the Parmesan into a mound on the baking sheet, then sprinkle one-quarter of the chopped walnuts over it. Tidy the edges slightly to make a circle about 4cm/1½in in diameter, then repeat to make 3 more circles, spacing them out by at least 5cm/2in as they tend to spread during cooking. Bake for 10 minutes until golden and crisp. Leave to cool for a few minutes before lifting them off the baking sheet with a palette knife and set aside.

3 Heat the olive oil and half of the butter in a large, ovenproof saucepan. Fry the onions, partially covered, for 10 minutes, stirring occasionally, until softened. Add the garlic and risotto rice and cook, stirring, for another 3 minutes until the rice is glossy and coated in the oil. Add the wine and cook, stirring, until it is absorbed by the rice. Add the stock, passata and sun-dried tomato paste and season with salt and pepper. Stir until well combined.

4 Cover the risotto with a tight-fitting, ovenproof lid and bake for 40 minutes, stirring once halfway through. Remove from the oven, stir in the remaining butter and set aside, covered, for 5 minutes.

5 Meanwhile, make the pesto. Put the remaining walnuts in a food processor and add the herbs and garlic. Process until coarsely chopped, then add the olive oil and process again to make a coarse paste. Transfer the mixture to a bowl and stir in the Parmesan, then season with salt and pepper.

6 Stir the risotto and divide it into 4 large, shallow bowls. Top with a good spoonful of the pesto and the shaved Parmesan and serve with the Parmesan crisps.

HERB RICOTTA FLAN WITH ROASTED TOMATO PESTO

Ricotta makes a light, summery flan but make sure you buy good quality cheese. The roasted tomato pesto is the perfect accompaniment, adding both colour and intense flavour. Serve the flan cut into wedges with new potatoes and a watercress salad.

SERVES 6

750g/1lb 10oz/3 cups ricotta cheese
85g/3oz/1 cup Parmesan, finely grated
3 large eggs, separated
4 tbsp torn basil leaves, plus whole leaves to garnish
4 tbsp oregano, plus extra to garnish
1 tsp salt, plus extra for seasoning
freshly ground black pepper

ROASTED TOMATO PESTO
4 tbsp pine nuts
400g/14oz cherry tomatoes
80ml/2½ fl oz/⅓ cup olive oil, plus extra for greasing
55g/2oz sun-blush tomatoes in oil (drained weight), coarsely chopped
1 garlic clove

1 Preheat the oven to 180°C/350°F/gas 4 and lightly grease a 20cm/8in loose-bottomed tin with a little of the olive oil. Put the ricotta, Parmesan and egg yolks in a food processor and blend until smooth and creamy. Transfer to a large mixing bowl and stir in the basil, oregano and salt and season with plenty of pepper.

2 Whisk the egg whites in a separate bowl until they form stiff peaks. Using a metal spoon, gently fold the egg whites into the ricotta mixture. Transfer the mixture to the tin and smooth the top with a palette knife. Bake on the lower rack of the oven for 30 minutes.

3 Meanwhile, put the cherry tomatoes for the pesto in a roasting tin with 2 tablespoons of the oil, season with salt and pepper and toss well. After the flan has been baking for 30 minutes, put the tomatoes in the top half of the oven above the flan and bake both for another 30 minutes until the flan is set and the top is light golden and the tomatoes have softened. Remove both from the oven. Leave the flan to cool slightly, then run a knife around the edge of the flan before removing from the tin.

4 To make the pesto, toast the pine nuts in a dry frying pan over a medium heat for 3–4 minutes, stirring occasionally, until lightly browned. Watch carefully so they do not burn. Remove from the heat and put half of them in a food processor. Add the roasted tomatoes, olive oil, sun-blush tomatoes, and garlic and process to a coarse paste, then season with salt and pepper.

5 Cut the flan into wedges and serve with the roasted tomato pesto, topped with the remaining basil, oregano and pine nuts.

CHESTNUT, STILTON AND ALE PUFF PASTRY PIE

This is a hearty pie for a cold winter's day. The Stilton melts into the ale sauce, enriching it and helping to create a thick gravy for the root vegetable and chestnut filling.

SERVES 4

1 tbsp olive oil
2 onions, coarsely chopped
1 celery stick, sliced
250g/9oz large, flat mushrooms, halved and thickly sliced
2 parsnips, peeled and cut into bite-sized chunks
225g/8oz Chantenay or baby carrots, trimmed (or 3 regular carrots, sliced)
150g/5½oz cooked chestnuts, thickly sliced
1 tsp dried thyme
200ml/7fl oz/scant 1 cup light ale
100ml/3½fl oz/scant ½ cup vegetable stock
2 tsp vegetarian Worcestershire sauce
2 tbsp plain flour, plus extra for rolling the pastry
100g/3½oz Stilton cheese, rind removed and coarsely chopped
280g/10oz puff pastry
plain flour, for rolling the pastry
1 egg, lightly beaten
salt and freshly ground black pepper

1 Preheat the oven to 200°C/400°F/gas 6. Heat the oil in a large pan over a medium-low heat and fry the onions, partially covered, for 10 minutes, stirring occasionally, until softened and golden. Add the celery, mushrooms, parsnips and carrots and sauté for 10 minutes, stirring often. Stir in the chestnuts and thyme.

2 Add the ale and bring to the boil, then reduce the heat to medium-low and cook for 3–5 minutes until reduced by half. Add the stock and Worcestershire sauce and return to a simmer. Mix together the flour and 1 tablespoon water and stir this mixture into the vegetables. Cook, stirring, for 5–10 minutes until the gravy has reduced and thickened. Add the Stilton, stir until combined and season to taste with salt and pepper.

3 Transfer the mixture to a 26 x 20cm/10½ x 8in ovenproof dish. Roll out the puff pastry on a lightly floured surface so that it is large enough to cover the dish. Wet the edge of the dish with water and lay the pastry on top of the filling, leaving a slight overhang. Trim off the excess pastry and use the back of a fork to seal the edges. Brush the top of the pie with egg and gently prick it in a few places with a fork. Bake for 35–40 minutes until risen and golden. Serve hot.

JERUSALEM ARTICHOKE, CELERIAC AND BLUE CHEESE TARTLETS

These individual tarts have a delicious crisp and buttery pastry base. Their free-form shape lends a rustic charm, which suits the earthy flavour of the root vegetable filling, but for a more refined look you could use small individual fluted tart tins.

MAKES 6

1 large Jerusalem artichoke, unpeeled and thinly sliced lengthways, outer slices discarded
1 tbsp olive oil, plus extra for greasing
450g/1lb celeriac, skin removed and cut into bite-sized chunks
50g/1¾ oz butter
100ml/3½ fl oz/scant ½ cup milk
2 tbsp chopped flat-leaf parsley leaves
70g/2½ oz dolcelatte or Cashel Blue cheese, crumbled
salt and freshly ground black pepper
1 recipe quantity Rosemary and Sea Salt Crushed Potatoes (see page 220), to serve

PASTRY

100g/3½ oz chilled butter, diced, plus extra for greasing
125g/4½ oz plain flour, sifted, plus extra for rolling the pastry
55ml/1¾ fl oz/scant ¼ cup soured cream

1 To make the pastry, put the butter and flour in a food processor and pulse until it resembles fine breadcrumbs. Add the soured cream and continue to pulse until the dough starts to come together. Remove the dough from the food processor, shape into a ball, wrap in cling film and chill for 30 minutes.

2 Grease the outer sides and base of six 150ml/5fl oz/scant ⅔ cup dariole moulds or ovenproof cups and put them upside down on a baking sheet. Roll out the pastry on a lightly floured work surface until about 5mm/¼ in thick. Cut out 6 circles, each about 11cm/4¼ in wide, and drape each one over the top of a dariole mould. Gently mould the pastry over the moulds to make 'cups' and chill for 30 minutes.

3 Preheat the oven to 200°C/400°F/gas 6, then bake the pastry cups for 30 minutes until light golden and crisp, then remove them from the moulds. Return the cups, right-side up, on the baking sheet, to the oven and bake for another 10 minutes. Transfer to a wire rack to cool.

4 While the pastry cups are baking, roast the Jerusalem artichoke. Lightly toss the artichoke slices in the olive oil and spread them out on a baking sheet. Bake for 30 minutes, turning once, until light golden and crisp in places.

5 Meanwhile, prepare the filling. Cook the celeriac in boiling salted water for 10 minutes or until tender. Drain well and return them to the pan. Add the butter and milk and warm through over a low heat, then transfer to a blender and purée until smooth and creamy. Season with salt and pepper and stir in the parsley.

6 Divide the celeriac purée into the pastry cups and top with the dolcelatte. Stand 1 slice of the roasted Jerusalem artichoke (you may have a few slices left over) upright in the middle of each tart and serve warm with roasted potatoes.

SWEET POTATO AND GOAT'S CHEESE GALETTES

Orange-fleshed sweet potatoes take on an almost caramel sweetness when baked, which goes well with the North African spices and crisp puff pastry base of these galettes.

SERVES 4

680g/1lb 8oz sweet potatoes
2 tbsp olive oil, plus extra for greasing
280g/10oz puff pastry
plain flour, for rolling the pastry
1 egg, lightly beaten
4 tbsp crème fraîche
1 red chilli, deseeded and finely sliced
2 tsp za'atar (see page 156) or cumin seeds
100g/3½oz goat's cheese, cut into chunks
1 small garlic clove, crushed
finely grated zest of 1 small lemon
2 tbsp chopped parsley leaves
salt and freshly ground black pepper

1 Preheat the oven to 200°C/400°F/gas 6. Bake the sweet potatoes for 40–45 minutes until tender. Set aside until cool enough to handle, then peel and cut into 5mm/¼in slices.

2 While the sweet potatoes are baking, grease a baking sheet with olive oil and set aside. Roll out the pastry on a lightly floured surface and cut it into 4 rectangles, each about 15 x 9cm/ 6 x 3½in. Put them on the baking sheet and brush with the egg, then, using a sharp knife, lightly score a border around each pastry base, about 1cm/½in from the edge.

3 Spread 1 tablespoon of the crème fraîche over each pastry rectangle, keeping it within the border. Arrange the slices of sweet potato, slightly overlapping, on top of the crème fraîche and sprinkle with the chilli and za'atar. Top with the goat's cheese and season with salt and pepper.

4 Bake the galettes for 25 minutes or until the pastry is golden. Take a peek under the galettes to make sure the base is cooked. Meanwhile, mix together the olive oil, garlic, lemon zest and parsley in a small bowl.

5 Drizzle the dressing over the galettes and serve.

OVEN-ROASTED RATATOUILLE IN TORTILLA BASKETS

Roasting concentrates the natural sugars in vegetables, enriching and enhancing their flavour and giving them a soft, almost caramelized texture.

SERVES 4

1 aubergine, sliced, then quartered

2 courgettes, thickly sliced

1 red pepper, deseeded and cut into 2.5cm/1in chunks

1 yellow pepper, deseeded and cut into 2.5cm/1in chunks

1 large fennel bulb, thickly sliced

2 onions, each cut into 6 wedges

3 large garlic cloves, thickly sliced

8 tomatoes, halved

100ml/3½ fl oz/scant ½ cup olive oil

3 rosemary sprigs

4 oregano sprigs

4 thyme sprigs

4 small soft flour tortillas

4 eggs, at room temperature

basil leaves, to decorate

salt and freshly ground black pepper

crème fraîche (optional), to serve

1 Preheat the oven to 220°C/425°F/gas 7. Put the aubergine, courgettes, red and yellow peppers, fennel, onions, garlic and tomatoes in a large bowl. Drizzle with the olive oil and toss well. Divide the vegetables on to two large baking trays and tuck in the rosemary, oregano and thyme. Roast for 20 minutes, then remove the herbs.

2 Turn the vegetables and return the trays to the oven, swapping them over. Roast for another 15 minutes until the vegetables are tender and caramelized in places. Season with salt and pepper, sprinkle with some basil leaves and set aside, covered, while you make the tortilla baskets.

3 Reduce the oven to 180°C/350°F/gas 4 and lightly grease four 300ml/10½ fl oz/1¼ cup ovenproof bowls (or mugs). Drape a tortilla over each bowl, gently pressing them down to form a cup shape. Put the bowls upside down on baking sheets and bake for 10 minutes or until the tortillas are golden and crisp, then leave to cool slightly.

4 Meanwhile, bring a small saucepan of water to the boil and carefully add the eggs. Return to the boil, then reduce the heat to medium and cook for 5 minutes. Remove the eggs from the pan and rinse under cold running water for 1 minute to stop them from cooking any further. Set aside and peel when cool enough to handle.

5 To serve, divide the ratatouille into the tortilla baskets. Cut the hard-boiled eggs in half lengthways and put 2 halves on top of each portion of ratatouille. Serve topped with crème fraîche, if desired.

POTATO, CELERIAC AND PORCINI MUSHROOM GRATIN

SERVES 4

20g/¾oz dried porcini mushrooms

30g/1oz butter

1 tbsp olive oil

3 garlic cloves, thinly sliced

300ml10½fl oz/scant 1¼ cups
   double cream

4 tbsp milk

300g/10½oz celeriac, peeled and
   cut into 5mm/¼in slices

550g/1lb 4oz potatoes, unpeeled,
   cut into 5mm/¼in slices

salt and freshly ground black pepper

1 Put the porcini mushrooms in a small bowl, cover with 100ml/
3½fl oz/scant ½ cup just boiled water and leave to soak for
20 minutes. Strain the soaking liquid into a clean bowl and set
aside, and then coarsely chop the mushrooms.

2 Heat the butter and olive oil in a large frying pan and fry the
garlic for 1 minute, stirring. Add the porcini and cook for another
1 minute, stirring. Add the mushroom soaking liquid to the pan. Add
the cream and milk, then season well with salt and pepper. Add the
celeriac and potatoes and gently turn to coat them in the creamy
mixture. Bring to the boil, then reduce the heat to low and simmer,
covered, for 20 minutes until the potatoes and celeriac are tender
but not too soft.

3 Meanwhile, preheat the oven to 220°C/425°F/gas 7. Transfer the
potato and celeriac mixture to a 26 x 20cm/10½ x 8in baking
dish and bake for 35 minutes or until the top is golden and the
vegetables are tender. Serve hot.

BAKED FONTINA, CARAWAY AND BUCKWHEAT PASTA

SERVES 4

2 potatoes, peeled and cubed

250g/9oz buckwheat penne

250g/9oz Savoy cabbage, shredded

3 tbsp olive oil, plus extra for
   greasing

1 large onion, finely chopped

2 garlic cloves, finely chopped

175g/6oz chestnut mushrooms,
   sliced

2 tsp caraway seeds

1 tsp cumin seeds

200ml/7fl oz/scant 1 cup hot
   vegetable stock

150g/5½oz Fontina cheese, cubed

25g/1oz/¼ cup coarsely chopped
   walnuts

salt and freshly ground black pepper

1 Preheat the oven to 200°C/400°F/gas 6 and grease a large, deep
baking dish with oil. Cook the potatoes in salted boiling water for
8 minutes or until just tender, then drain and set aside.

2 Meanwhile, cook the pasta in boiling salted water until it is just
cooked and remains al dente (about 2 minutes less than stated on
the packet instructions). Add the Savoy cabbage in the last minute
of cooking, then drain and rinse under cold running water to stop
the cooking process.

3 Heat the olive oil in a large, non-stick saucepan over a medium-
low heat. Fry the onions for 8 minutes, stirring occasionally, until
golden and softened. Add the garlic, mushrooms and caraway and
cumin seeds and cook for another 4 minutes until tender.

4 Remove the pan from the heat and add the potatoes, pasta,
cabbage and stock. Stir until combined, then season with salt and
pepper. Transfer to the baking dish and top with the Fontina and
walnuts. Bake for 20 minutes until the cheese is bubbling and
golden, then serve.

PARMESAN ROULADE WITH KABOCHA SQUASH

The beauty of a roulade is that is can be prepared in advance – and despite its impressive appearance, it's relatively easy to make. Serve with a rocket and spinach salad, if desired. If you can't find kabocha, you can also use acorn or butternut squash.

SERVES 6

55g/2oz butter
55g/2oz/scant ½ cup plain flour
310ml/10¾ fl oz/1¼ cups milk
70g/2½ oz mature Cheddar cheese, grated
55g/2oz Parmesan cheese, finely-grated
4 eggs, separated
salt and freshly ground black pepper

FILLING

300g/10½ oz kabocha squash, peeled, deseeded and diced
3 garlic cloves
2 tbsp cream cheese
1 heaped tsp Dijon mustard
1 handful of coriander leaves, chopped
1 handful of flat-leaf parsley leaves, chopped

1 Preheat the oven to 190°C/375°F/gas 5 and line a 30 x 23cm/ 12 x 9in baking tray with baking paper. Melt the butter in a large non-stick saucepan. Add the flour and cook, stirring continuously, for 1 minute. Gradually stir in the milk. Bring to the boil, stirring, until the sauce is thick and smooth. Remove from the heat and stir in the Cheddar and three-quarters of the Parmesan until melted. Beat in the egg yolks and season with salt and pepper.

2 In a large, clean bowl, whisk the egg whites until they form stiff peaks. Fold a spoonful of the egg whites into the cheese sauce, then fold in the rest until incorporated, taking care not to lose too much volume. Pour the mixture into the baking tray and gently spread out into an even layer. Bake for 15 minutes or until risen and golden.

3 Meanwhile, steam the squash for 5 minutes, then add the garlic and continue steaming for another 5 minutes until tender. Purée the squash, garlic, cream cheese and mustard in a blender, then set aside to cool.

4 Sprinkle the remaining Parmesan over a sheet of baking paper about the same size as the baking tray. Remove the roulade from the oven, turn it out on to the paper and peel off the paper lining it was baked on. Trim and discard the crisp outer edges of the roulade.

5 Spread the squash mixture over the roulade. Sprinkle the coriander and parsley leaves lengthways down the centre and season with salt and pepper. Using the baking paper to help guide you, roll up the roulade from the short end as tightly as possible to form a log. Discard the paper, cut the roulade into slices and serve.

ROSEMARY AND SEA SALT CRUSHED POTATOES

These crisp, golden new potatoes (pictured, page 212) make an excellent alternative to traditional roast spuds. Make sure the potatoes are about the same size so they cook evenly.

SERVES 6

1kg/2lb 4oz new potatoes, scrubbed, whole and unpeeled
2 tbsp olive oil
40g/1 ½ oz butter, cut into small pieces
2 long rosemary sprigs
salt flakes

1 Preheat the oven to 220°C/425°F/gas 7. Boil the potatoes for 15 minutes until partially cooked, then drain well.
2 Put the olive oil in a large roasting tin and heat in the oven for 3 minutes. Using the back of a fork, crush the top of each potato – they should keep their shape but have a 'cracked' top half. Arrange the potatoes in the tin in a single layer, spaced slightly apart.
3 Put a small piece of the butter on top of each potato and sprinkle with a few flakes of salt. Roast the potatoes for 20 minutes.
4 Pull the leaves off the rosemary in small sprigs and insert 2 or 3 into the top of each potato. Roast for another 15–20 minutes, until crisp and golden, then serve.

PARMESAN-CRUSTED PARSNIPS

Finely grated Parmesan cheese gives these roasted parsnips a delightful golden crust.

SERVES 4

300g/10 ½ oz parsnips, peeled and halved or quartered, if large
40g/1 ½ oz Parmesan cheese, finely grated
55g/2oz/scant ½ cup plain flour
2 tbsp olive oil
20g/¾ oz butter
salt and freshly ground black pepper

1 Preheat the oven to 190°C/375°F/gas 5. Boil the parsnips for 3 minutes until slightly tender.
2 Meanwhile, mix together the Parmesan and flour in a large bowl and season with salt and pepper.
3 Drain the parsnips and while still hot and steamy toss them, a few at a time, in the Parmesan mixture until coated.
4 Put half of the olive oil in a large baking tray and heat it in the oven for 2 minutes. Meanwhile, heat the butter and remaining oil in a small saucepan until melted. Arrange the parsnips in the tray in a single layer and brush the tops with the butter and oil mixture. Roast for 40 minutes, turning once, until golden and crisp all over, then serve.

BAKED VEGETABLES IN A BAG

The baking parchment parcels help to retain the juices from the vegetables while they cook, preventing them from drying out and producing a fresh and simple sauce. You could also top the vegetables with a spoonful of pesto and a few shavings of Parmesan just before serving, if you like.

SERVES 4

2 tbsp olive oil
2 tbsp verjuice or white wine vinegar
2 red onions, peeled and each cut into 6 wedges with the stem intact
8 large garlic cloves
1 fennel bulb, cut into wedges
2 courgettes, halved and cut into batons
2 handfuls of cherry tomatoes
1 small handful of basil leaves
salt and freshly ground black pepper

1 Preheat the oven 190°C/375°F/gas 5. Mix together the olive oil and verjuice in a large bowl. Add the onions, garlic, fennel, courgettes and tomatoes and turn them until coated in the olive oil mixture.

2 Take 2 large sheets of baking paper and divide the vegetables between them, placing them in the centre. Season the vegetables with salt and pepper and top with a few basil leaves. Gather up the paper and secure to make 2 parcels, either by securing with string or folding the edges over to seal. Put the parcels in baking trays and roast for 45 minutes or until the vegetables are tender.

3 Carefully open the parcels and remove the cooked basil leaves. Top with basil leaves and serve.

ROASTED GARLIC WITH CHARGRILLED TOAST

Roasted garlic takes on a subtle flavour and loses its harsh pungency. It also takes on a wonderful creamy texture, making it almost spreadable.

SERVES 4

2 garlic bulbs
1 tbsp olive oil, plus extra for drizzling
4 thick slices of rustic-style bread
salt and freshly ground black pepper

1 Preheat the oven to 180°C/350°F/gas 4. Slice the top of each bulb of garlic so the cloves are just exposed. Put each bulb on a piece of foil large enough to make a parcel. Drizzle with the olive oil and pull up the foil to loosely enclose.

2 Put the parcels in a baking tray and roast for 30–40 minutes or until the cloves are soft and tender. When cool enough to handle, squeeze the softened cloves out of the skins and into a small bowl.

3 Heat a griddle pan over a medium heat and toast both sides of the bread until blackened in places. Spread the garlic over each slice, season with salt and pepper and drizzle with a little more oil, then serve.

ROASTED BALSAMIC PEARS

Roasted until tender and slightly caramelized, the pears make a great accompaniment to the Mushroom and Cashew Pies (see page 204).

SERVES 4

4 pears
1 tbsp lemon juice
2 tbsp balsamic vinegar
1 tbsp olive oil
salt and freshly ground black pepper

1 Preheat the oven to 200°C/400°F/gas 6. Peel the pears and halve them lengthways, then brush with the lemon juice to prevent them from discolouring.
2 Mix together the balsamic vinegar and olive oil and season with salt and pepper. Brush the pears with the balsamic mixture, put them on a baking tray and roast for 30–35 minutes until tender and golden, then serve.

AUBERGINE CAVIAR

This version of the Middle Eastern classic aubergine dish, baba ganoush, is baked in the oven until meltingly soft.

SERVES 4

2 aubergines
2 garlic cloves, crushed
juice of 1 large lemon
2 tbsp light tahini
1 tsp ground cumin
4 tbsp natural yogurt
salt and freshly ground black pepper

1 Preheat the oven to 220°C/425°F/gas 7. Prick the aubergines all over and put them on a baking sheet. Roast for 45–50 minutes until the inside is meltingly soft.
2 Scoop out the aubergine flesh, discarding the skin, and chop finely. Transfer the chopped aubergine to a bowl and stir in the garlic, lemon juice, tahini, cumin and yogurt until smooth and creamy. Season with salt and pepper to taste and serve.

ROASTED PLUM VERRINES WITH TOFFEE PECANS

Verrines are individual layered glassfuls of deliciousness – in this case a sweetened rosewater cream, slow-roasted spiced plums, amaretti biscuits and toffee-coated pecans. The desserts can be made a few hours in advance and chilled, but bring them back to room temperature before serving.

SERVES 4

250ml/9fl oz/1 cup whipping cream
2 tbsp icing sugar
1 tsp rosewater
8 amaretti biscuits, broken

SLOW-ROASTED PLUMS

170ml/5½fl oz/²⁄₃ cup freshly
   squeezed orange juice
1 tsp lemon juice
½ tsp cinnamon
2 cloves
1 star anise
2 tbsp caster sugar
200g/7oz plums, halved and pitted

TOFFEE PECANS

2 tbsp butter
3 tbsp granulated sugar
150g/5½oz/scant 1½ cup pecan
   halves

1 To make the plums, mix together the orange and lemon juice, cinnamon, cloves, star anise and caster sugar in a large bowl. Add the plums and turn until soaked. Remove the plums from the bowl reserving the orange juice mixture, and arrange them, cut-side down, on a baking sheet. Put the plums in a cold oven, turn it on and set the temperature to 160°C/315°F/gas 3. Cook for 1 hour until slightly shrivelled and softened.

2 About 10 minutes before the plums are ready, put the orange juice mixture in a saucepan and bring to the boil. Reduce the heat to low and simmer for 5–8 minutes until thickened and syrupy. Remove the pan from the heat, add the roasted plums and leave to cool. Remove and discard the whole spices.

3 Meanwhile, make the toffee pecans. Line a baking sheet with baking paper. Melt the butter in a small, non-stick frying pan and add the granulated sugar. Stir over a medium-low heat for 5 minutes or until the sugar melts and turns golden. Remove from the heat and add the pecans, stirring until coated in the syrup, then spoon on to the baking sheet, spreading them apart. Leave to cool.

4 Whip the cream until it forms soft peaks, then whisk in the icing sugar and rosewater. Roughly chop three-quarters of the pecans and mix with the broken amaretti biscuits.

5 In four glasses, arrange layers of the amaretti and pecan mixture, rosewater cream and plums with a little bit of their syrup. Top each portion with more cream and a few of the reserved pecans and serve.

MAPLE FIGS WITH CARDAMOM SHORTBREAD

You want lovely just-ripe figs for this recipe — not too soft or they will lose their shape during baking.

SERVES 4–6

12 figs
5 tbsp maple syrup
½ tsp cinnamon
3 tbsp freshly squeezed orange juice
zest of 1 orange
20g/¾ oz butter
170ml/5½ fl oz/⅔ cup Greek yogurt, to serve

CARDAMOM SHORTBREAD

100g/3½ oz butter, softened, plus extra for greasing
50g/1¾ oz/scant ½ cup icing sugar, plus extra for dusting
a pinch of salt
100g/3½ oz/heaped ¾ cup plain flour, sifted, plus extra for rolling the dough
50g/1¾ oz/heaped ¼ cup rice flour or cornflour, sifted
seeds from 5 cardamom pods, crushed
caster sugar, for dusting

1 First, make the cardamom shortbread. Preheat the oven to 160°C/315°F/gas 3 and lightly grease a 20 x 12cm/8 x 4½in baking tin (or section of a baking tray, as the shortbread keeps its shape during baking). Using an electric mixer, cream the butter and icing sugar together for 6–8 minutes until light and fluffy, then add the salt, both flours and cardamom seeds and beat until incorporated. Using your hands, press the mixture together to form a smooth ball of dough, then wrap in cling film and chill for 30 minutes.

2 Roll out the dough on a lightly floured surface to about 1.5cm/⅝in thick. It will be quite crumbly but don't worry. Press it into the tin and bake for 25–30 minutes until pale golden and crisp. Dust the shortbread with the caster sugar and cut into 8 fingers, each 12cm/4½in long, and leave to cool in the tin while you prepare the figs.

3 Increase the oven temperature to 190°C/375°F/gas 5. Using a small, sharp knife, cut a cross in the top of each fig, cutting halfway down to the base. Stand the figs upright in a roasting tin, opening them out slightly, and set aside.

4 Put the maple syrup, cinnamon, orange juice and zest, and butter in a saucepan and bring to the boil, then reduce the heat to low. Cook, stirring continuously, for 3–5 minutes, until syrupy and thickened. Spoon the sauce over the figs and bake for 10–15 minutes until softened. Serve the figs warm or at room temperature with any juices in the pan and with the shortbread fingers and yogurt.

VEGAN CHOCOLATE CAKE WITH MAPLE DRIZZLE

This cake is amazing – it's a wonder that it works and it does so with great results! A doddle to make, you simply just mix everything together and it holds together and rises perfectly, even though there are no eggs or butter.

SERVES 12

80ml/2½ fl oz/⅓ cup sunflower oil, plus extra for greasing
225g/8oz/1¾ cups plain flour
225g/8oz/scant 1 cup caster sugar
1 tsp bicarbonate of soda
½ tsp salt
3 tbsp cocoa powder
1 tsp vanilla extract
1 tbsp distilled vinegar or white vinegar

MAPLE DRIZZLE

90g/3¼ oz/⅓ cup vegan cream cheese
40g/1½ oz/⅓ cup icing sugar
1 tsp vanilla extract
1 tbsp maple syrup

1 Preheat the oven to 180°/350°F/gas 4 and lightly grease a 450g/1lb loaf tin with sunflower oil.

2 In a large bowl, sift together the flour, sugar, bicarbonate of soda, salt and cocoa powder, mixing until combined. In a separate bowl, mix together the oil, vanilla extract, vinegar and 250ml/9fl oz/1 cup water. Add the wet mixture to the dry ingredients and stir until smooth.

3 Pour the mixture into the tin and bake for 45–50 minutes until risen – a skewer inserted in the centre of the cake should come out clean. Leave to cool for 5 minutes before turning out of the tin on to a wire rack to cool completely.

4 To make the maple drizzle, beat together the cream cheese, icing sugar, vanilla extract and maple syrup until smooth. Chill for 30 minutes to thicken slightly. Cut the cake into slices, drizzle each slice with a spoonful of the maple icing and serve.

PEAR, BANANA AND CHOCOLATE WONTONS

SERVES 4

sunflower oil, for greasing

16 wonton wrappers

½ small just-ripe pear (not too
soft), peeled, halved and thinly
sliced

55g/2oz dark chocolate, broken or
chopped into 8 equal pieces

1 small banana, sliced

25g/1oz butter, melted

icing sugar, for dusting

1 Preheat the oven to 190°C/375°F/gas 5 and lightly grease two
baking sheets with sunflower oil. Put 1 wonton wrapper on a work
surface and put 1 slice of the pear and 1 chunk of the chocolate in
the centre. Brush the edges of the wrapper with water and cover
with a second wrapper. Press the edges together to seal, then put
the wonton parcel on the baking sheet. Repeat to make 3 more
pear and chocolate wonton parcels, then make 4 more parcels
using the banana and the remaining chocolate (you will have some
fruit leftover).

2 Brush the parcels with the melted butter and bake for 10 minutes
until golden and crisp.

3 Dust the parcels with a little icing sugar and serve, allowing one
banana and one pear wonton per person.

PUMPKIN CHEESECAKE

SERVES 8–10

200g/7oz pumpkin or kabocha
squash, deseeded and cut into
wedges

300g/10½oz/1¼ cups cream
cheese

250g/9oz/1 cup ricotta

225g/8oz/scant 1 cup caster sugar

2 tsp vanilla extract

3 eggs

whole nutmeg, for grating

finely sliced zest of 1 unwaxed
lemon, to decorate

single cream, to serve

BASE

125g/4½oz digestive biscuits

50g/1¾oz/scant ½ cup ground
almonds

60g/2¼oz butter, melted, plus extra
for greasing

1 Preheat the oven to 200°C/400°F/gas 6. Grease the sides of a deep
20cm/8in springform cake tin with melted butter and line the base
with baking paper. Stand the pumpkin wedges on a baking tray and
roast for 25–30 minutes until tender, then remove from the oven
and reduce the oven temperature to 150°C/300°F/gas 2.

2 Meanwhile, make the base. Put the digestive biscuits in a food
processor and pulse until fine, then transfer to a bowl and mix in
the almonds and butter until combined. Press the mixture in an
even layer into the base of the tin and chill until required.

3 Remove and discard the skin from the pumpkin and purée the flesh
in a food processor or blender for a few seconds until smooth. Press
the purée through a sieve to remove any fibres.

4 Put the cream cheese and ricotta in the food processor and blend
until smooth, then add the pumpkin purée, caster sugar, vanilla
extract and eggs and process again until combined. Pour the
mixture on to the base and bake for 1 hour 10 minutes or until
set but still a little wobbly. Remove from the oven and leave the
cheesecake to cool in the tin.

5 Grate a generous amount of nutmeg over the cheesecake, sprinkle
with the lemon zest and serve with single cream.

CHOCOLATE TRUFFLE TORTE WITH AMARETTO CREAM

This rich and indulgent cake is slightly gooey in the centre, its intense chocolate truffle topping complemented by the crisp amaretti and roasted hazelnut base. The amaretto-infused cream makes a decadent accompaniment, while fresh strawberries or raspberries are perfect partners too.

SERVES 10–12

175g/6oz dark chocolate, broken into chunks
140g/4¾oz unsalted butter
175g/6oz/¾ cup caster sugar
4 large eggs, separated
1 tsp vanilla extract
85g/3oz/scant 1 cup ground almonds
cocoa powder, for dusting

HAZELNUT AND AMARETTI BASE

plain flour, for greasing
60g/2¼oz/heaped ¼ cup whole skinned hazelnuts
175g/6oz amaretti biscuits
60g/2¼oz butter, plus extra for greasing
plain flour, for greasing

AMARETTO CREAM

300ml/10½fl oz/scant 1¼ cups whipping cream
1 tbsp amaretto liqueur, or to taste
1 tbsp icing sugar, or to taste

1 First, make the base. Preheat the oven to 180°C/350°F/gas 4. Lightly grease and flour the sides of a 20cm/8in springform cake tin and line the base with baking paper. Put the hazelnuts on a baking tray and roast for 6–7 minutes, until lightly toasted. Remove from the oven and leave to cool.

2 Put the hazelnuts and amaretti biscuits in a food processor and pulse until finely ground. Melt the butter in a medium saucepan over a medium-low heat. Remove from the heat and stir in the biscuits and nuts until combined. Press the biscuit mixture into the base of the cake tin to make a firm, even layer. Set aside while you make the truffle filling.

3 Put the chocolate in a heatproof bowl and rest it over a pan of gently simmering water, making sure the bottom of the bowl does not touch the water. Heat for 4–5 minutes, stirring occasionally, until the chocolate has melted, then set aside to cool slightly.

4 Cream the caster sugar and butter in a mixing bowl until light and fluffy. Beat in the egg yolks, one at a time, then beat in the vanilla extract and melted chocolate. When thoroughly blended, mix in the ground almonds.

5 In a clean bowl, whisk the egg whites until they form stiff peaks, then fold them into the cake mixture in three batches and pour the mixture over the base. Bake for 40–45 minutes until cooked on the outside but still slightly runny in the centre. Don't worry if it cracks a little. Remove from the oven and leave to cool in the tin.

6 To make the amaretto cream, whip the cream in a clean bowl until it starts to thicken, then add the liqueur and icing sugar. Continue whipping until soft peaks form. Taste and add more liqueur or sugar, if you like.

7 Dust the cake with a layer of cocoa powder and serve with a large spoonful of the amaretto cream.

CARAMELIZED LEMON AND ALMOND TART

Tangy with an intense lemon flavour, this tart has a golden caramelized top and a spelt pastry case. Spelt is an ancient form of wheat and produces a slightly nutty-flavoured pastry, but you could also use plain flour.

SERVES 8
2 eggs
50g/1¾oz/scant ¼ cup caster
    sugar
finely grated zest and juice
    of 4 unwaxed lemons
1 tsp vanilla extract
55g/2oz ground almonds
125ml/4fl oz/½ cup single cream
3 tbsp icing sugar

PASTRY
225g/8oz/scant 1¾ cups spelt
    flour, plus extra for rolling the
    pastry
70g/2½oz/heaped ½ cup icing
    sugar
a pinch of salt
125g/4½oz chilled butter, plus
    extra for greasing
1 egg, lightly beaten

1 First make the pastry. Sift the flour, icing sugar and salt into a mixing bowl. Rub in the butter with your fingertips until the mixture resembles fine breadcrumbs, then add the egg and mix to combine. Press the dough together to make a smooth ball, then flatten into a disc, wrap in cling film and chill for 20 minutes.

2 Lightly grease a 23cm/9in loose-bottomed flan tin with butter. Roll out the dough on a lightly floured surface and then press it gently into the tin. Prick the pastry case all over with a fork and chill for 15 minutes.

3 Preheat the oven to 180°C/350°F/gas 4. Line the pastry case with baking paper and fill with baking beans, then bake for 10 minutes. Remove the baking beans and paper and bake for another 10 minutes until light golden.

4 Meanwhile, make the filling. Put the eggs and caster sugar in a large bowl and whisk with an electric hand-whisk for 5–7 minutes until the mixture is pale and thickened enough to leave a trail when the whisk is lifted. Stir in the lemon zest and juice, vanilla extract, ground almonds and cream. Pour the filling into the pastry case and bake for 25 minutes or until set.

5 Heat the grill to high. Sift the icing sugar evenly over the tart and grill for 1–2 minutes, until the sugar melts and caramelizes – watch carefully to make sure it doesn't burn. Leave the tart to cool slightly. Serve warm or at room temperature.

RHUBARB AND CUSTARD TARTLETS

These pretty tartlets are made with sour cream pastry, which has a light and flaky texture and holds together well when rolled out. The rhubarb is baked until soft and slightly caramelized.

MAKES 10
250ml/9fl oz/1 cup milk
5 tbsp single cream
1 large egg
1 egg yolk
60g/2 ¼ oz/heaped ¼ cup caster
    sugar
1 tsp vanilla extract

SOURED CREAM PASTRY
100g/3 ½ oz cold butter, diced, plus
    extra for greasing
125g/4 ½ oz/1 cup plain flour, sifted,
    plus extra for rolling the dough
55ml/1 ¾ fl oz/scant ¼ cup soured
    cream

RHUBARB
25g/1oz butter
5 tbsp maple syrup
300g/10 ½ oz rhubarb, cut into
    2.5cm/1in pieces

1 To make the soured cream pastry, put the butter and flour in a food processor and pulse until it resembles fine breadcrumbs. Add the soured cream and continue pulsing until the dough starts to come together. Remove the dough from the food processor, shape into a ball, wrap in cling film and chill for 30 minutes.

2 Preheat the oven to 180°C/350°F/gas 4 and grease 10 holes of a deep muffin tin with butter. Roll out the pastry on a lightly floured work surface to about 3mm/⅛ in thick. Cut out 10 rounds, slightly larger than the muffin cups and press them gently into the muffin tin. Chill for 30 minutes.

3 Gently heat the milk and cream in a small saucepan until almost boiling. In a bowl, whisk together the egg, egg yolk, caster sugar and vanilla extract until pale, then gradually whisk in the milk mixture. Leave to cool.

4 Pour the egg mixture evenly into the pastry cups and bake for 30–35 minutes until the pastry is golden and the custard is just set.

5 Meanwhile, cook the rhubarb. Melt the butter in a non-stick pan over a medium-low heat, add the maple syrup, then the rhubarb. Turn the rhubarb in the hot syrup mixture for 2 minutes. Arrange the rhubarb pieces in an even layer on a non-stick baking sheet and spoon a little of the syrup mixture over them. Bake for 25 minutes, turning once and spooning a little more of the syrup over them, until tender and slightly caramelized.

6 Remove the tartlets and rhubarb from the oven. Leave the tartlets to cool in the tin, then transfer to a wire rack. Leave the rhubarb to cool. Top the tartlets with some of the rhubarb and serve.

MERINGUE WITH TOASTED HAZELNUTS AND BUTTERSCOTCH SAUCE

This meringue is cooked at a higher temperature than usual, so the addition of cornflour and vinegar in the mixture gives it a delicious combination of gooey middle and crisp outer shell. The result is a perfect marriage of marshmallow-centred meringue, toasted hazelnuts, vanilla cream, rich butterscotch sauce and fresh raspberries.

SERVES 6–8

70g/2½oz/scant ½ cup hazelnuts

5 large egg whites

300g/10½oz/scant 1⅔ cups caster sugar

1 tsp cornflour

1 tsp white wine vinegar

400ml/14fl oz/ 1½ cups plus 2 tbsp double cream

1 tsp vanilla extract

175g/6oz/heaped 1⅓ cup fresh raspberries

BUTTERSCOTCH SAUCE

200ml/7fl oz/scant 1 cup golden syrup

3 tbsp caster sugar

3 tbsp soft light brown sugar

60g/2¼ oz butter

125ml/4fl oz/½ cup double cream

1 Preheat the oven to 180°C/350°F/gas 4. Roast the hazelnuts in a baking tray for 6–8 minutes or until toasted, taking care as they can easily burn. Transfer the nuts into a clean tea towel, gather up the edges to make a bundle and rub the nuts to remove the skins. Leave to cool, then coarsely chop.

2 Whisk the egg whites in a clean bowl until they form stiff peaks. Add the caster sugar a little bit at a time, whisking after each addition. Continue whisking for 3–4 minutes until the mixture is stiff and glossy, then whisk in the vinegar and cornflour.

3 Line a large baking sheet with baking paper. Heap the meringue into a rough 20cm/8in round on the baking sheet and make a slight well in the centre. Bake in the centre of the oven for 40–45 minutes until light golden and crisp on the outside but still soft in the centre. Turn the oven off, open the door and leave the meringue inside to cool completely.

4 Meanwhile, make the butterscotch sauce. Put the syrup, caster sugar, brown sugar and butter in a saucepan and bring to the boil, then reduce the heat to low and cook, stirring occasionally, for 5 minutes until thickened. Remove from the heat and stir in the cream. Leave to cool and thicken.

5 Transfer the meringue to a serving plate. Just before serving, whip the cream and vanilla extract together until soft peaks form, then heap it on top of the meringue. Sprinkle with the toasted hazelnuts and drizzle with the butterscotch sauce (you will have some left over). Sprinkle the raspberries over the top and serve.

PINEAPPLE AND COCONUT SOUFFLÉS

Soufflés have a reputation for being tricky to make but this one couldn't be more well-behaved, producing a light and fluffy dessert with a touch of the Caribbean.

SERVES 4

3 tbsp desiccated coconut

butter, for greasing

3 large eggs, separated

70g/2 ½ oz/scant ⅓ cup caster sugar

200g/7oz tinned pineapple in natural juice, drained and finely chopped

icing sugar, for dusting

1 Preheat the oven to 190°C/375°F/gas 5 and lightly butter four 150ml/5fl oz/scant ⅔ cup ramekins with butter. Put half of the coconut on a baking sheet and toast in the oven for 2 minutes until golden, then set aside.

2 Whisk together the egg yolks and half of the caster sugar for 5–7 minutes until light and fluffy. Stir in the pineapple and the untoasted coconut and set aside.

3 Whisk the egg whites in a clean bowl until stiff peaks form, then add the remaining caster sugar in two batches, continuing to whisk until thick and glossy. Gradually and gently fold the mixture into the pineapple mixture, taking care not to lose too much volume.

4 Spoon the soufflé mixture into the ramekins, filling them to the brim, and smooth the tops with a palette knife. Bake for 10 minutes until risen and golden. Sift a little icing sugar over the top, sprinkle with the toasted coconut and serve immediately.

APPLE, HONEY AND ROSEMARY CLAFOUTIS

This classic French pudding is given a twist with the addition of honey and a hint of fresh rosemary.

SERVES 6

170ml/5 ½ fl oz/⅔ cup milk

125ml/4fl oz/½ cup double cream

5cm/2in rosemary sprig

3 tbsp clear honey

butter, for greasing

3 eggs

a pinch of salt

80g/2 ¾ oz/⅓ cup caster sugar

40g/1 ½ oz/⅓ cup plain flour

2 apples, peeled, cored, halved and thinly sliced

icing sugar, for dusting

1 Put the milk, cream, rosemary and honey in a medium saucepan and stir well. Bring to the boil, then remove from the heat and leave to infuse for 25 minutes. Remove and discard the rosemary.

2 Preheat the oven to 180°C/350°F/gas 4 and lightly grease a 26 x 20cm/10 ½ x 8in baking dish with butter. In a large bowl, whisk the eggs, salt and caster sugar for 6–8 minutes until pale, fluffy and more than doubled in volume. Fold in the flour and then the milk mixture. Pour the mixture into the baking dish and arrange the apple slices over the top – they will sink slightly into the batter.

3 Bake for 35 minutes or until risen and golden. Sift a little icing sugar over the top and serve warm.

INDEX